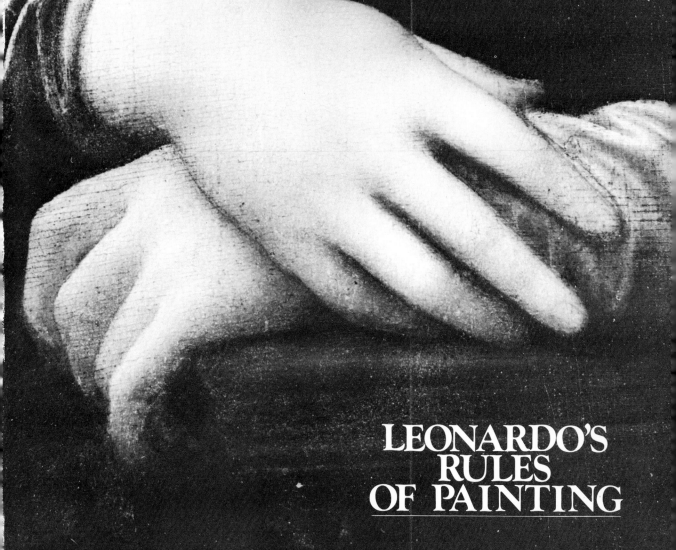

LEONARDO'S RULES OF PAINTING

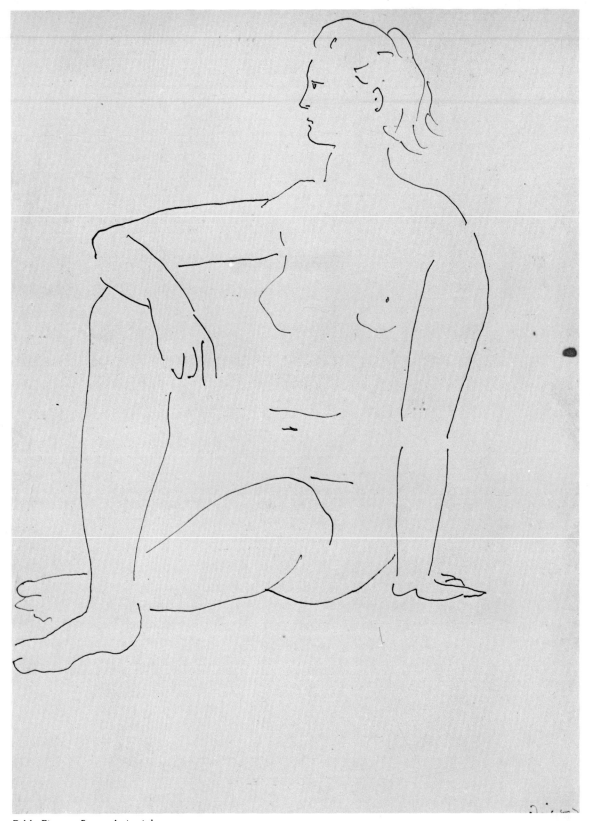

Pablo Picasso, *Femme Assise*, ink on paper.

LEONARDO'S RULES OF PAINTING

An Unconventional Approach to Modern Art

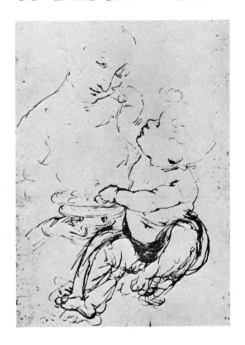

James Beck

·A Studio Book·

·The Viking Press·

·New York·

As is always the case with a book of this kind, a number of colleagues and friends played important roles in shaping its final form. I am indebted to Amy Golahny, Jeanne Plekon, and Francis Preston for general assistance of many kinds; to Jennifer Licht and Roberta Bernstein for excellent suggestions about illustrations; to Martina D'Alton and Barbara Burn for superb editorial and practical advice; to Amy Pershing, who good-naturedly and efficiently carried the main burden of seeing the book through the press.

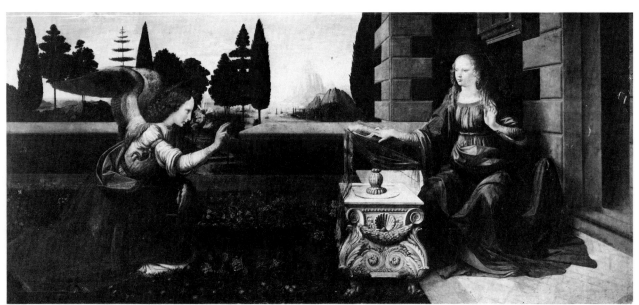

Leonardo da Vinci, *Annunciation*,
c. 1476, oil on panel,
cm. 98 x 217.

First published in 1979 by
The Viking Press/A Studio Book
625 Madison Avenue, New York, N.Y. 10022
Published simultaneously in Canada by
Penguin Books Canada Limited

Library of Congress Cataloging in Publication Data
Beck, James.
   Leonardo's rules of painting.
   (A Studio book)
   1. Leonardo da Vinci, 1452–1519.   2. Painting—Philosophy.   3. Painting—Technique.   4. Leonardo da Vinci, 1452–1519—Influence.   I. Title.
   ND623.L5B4   759.5   79-13220
   ISBN 0-670-42427-7

Printed in the United States of America

Designed by Michael Shroyer

Contents

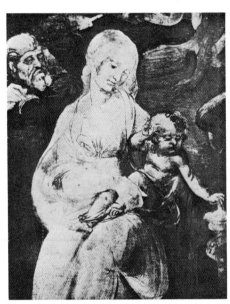

Leonardo da Vinci, *Adoration of the Magi* (detail),
1481, oil, underpainting on panel,
cm. 246.5 x 243.5.

Preface

Leonardo da Vinci's ideas about painting have significance for modern and contemporary art, although the statement may seem improbable. My purpose in this book is to demonstrate the connection by selecting a number of Leonardo's statements about art and setting them beside paintings and drawings by modern artists. The juxtapositions, which essentially speak for themselves, confirm for me the premise that the observations Leonardo made at the end of the fifteenth century and the beginning of the sixteenth have relevance and validity today. I suppose that the argument might even be carried one step further: many of the ideas and precepts expressed by Leonardo have permanent and universal validity.

I do not mean to suggest that modern artists have sought specifically to follow the precepts found in Leonardo's writings, although the possibility should not be excluded. Certain ideas that can be at least indirectly connected with Leonardo and his Renaissance contemporaries have entered into the mainstream of artistic thinking and studio practice. Furthermore, many recent painters have had a special admiration for Leonardo and are well acquainted with the ideas he expressed.

In selecting the quotations and even in establishing categories I have not sought completeness, or a fully balanced selection, if only because Leonardo's notebooks are not complete as preserved. Undeniably, Leonardo planned to write a treatise on painting for publication, and this would have served to broadcast his ideas. Some of his earliest preserved notes (c. 1490–1492) contain material for such a work, and although they are "early" in terms of his extant writings, they represent the thoughts of a man nearly forty who had enormous experience in various artistic endeavors. Leonardo's projected treatise was based on his own investigations and conclusions rather than on precepts found in compilations or hand-

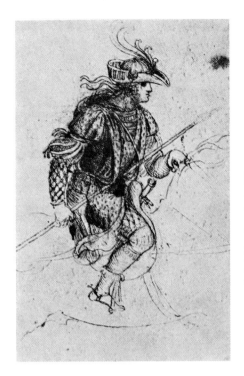

books dating either from the previous decades of the fifteenth century or from antiquity. The mathematician Luca Pacioli, a fellow central Italian in the Milanese court when Leonardo was there, mentioned that by 1498 Leonardo had finished a written work on painting and on human motion. Leonardo apparently was not content with the work, however, and continued to expand and perfect his ideas on the subject, much as he reworked paintings over a long period of time.

The work known as Leonardo's *Treatise on Painting* did not exist at the time of his death in 1519. Thanks to the efforts of his heir and follower Francesco Melzi, a treatise extracted from the body of Leonardo's writings was prepared for publication between 1525 and 1530. (The actual publication of an edition, however, had to wait until the middle of the seventeenth century.) Leonardo's precise intentions, the order and the arrangement of his ideas, and the eventual revisions he might have made in the *Treatise on Painting* are impossible to ascertain. Scholars have tried with great ingenuity to reconstruct the chronology of the notebooks and to determine accurate dates for one or another idea, but technical questions of this sort are largely unanswerable and irrelevant to the theme of this book.* Leonardo's ideas circulated among artists by word of mouth as well as by manuscript and the printed page and have been published over the centuries in various languages and in abridged form. They have enjoyed a steady popularity, judging from the number of editions that have been printed.

Leonardo's ideas about painting are not fully represented by the *Treatise on Painting;* many are found scattered throughout his notebooks and in the Codex

*For a full account of the history of the *Treatise on Painting,* see Carlo Pedretti, *Commentary on the Literary Works of Leonardo da Vinci,* compiled and edited by Jean Paul Richter (Oxford and Los Angeles, 1977), I, pp. 12 ff.

Atlanticus* but were never incorporated into the *Treatise*. For this reason, I have not limited the quotations in this book to items from the *Treatise*, although by far the largest number come from that source. Rather, the entire body of Leonardo's preserved notes was used as a reservoir, including the newly discovered manuscripts in Madrid. I have used the edition translated and annotated by A. Philip McMahon (Leonardo da Vinci, *Treatise on Painting*, Princeton, 1956, two volumes) and have employed the following system of reference to it: [McM., no. 1] means the McMahon edition, item number 1. Edward MacCurdy's edition and translation of the *Notebooks of Leonardo* (New York, n.d., two volumes in one) is cited as [MacC.], followed by a page reference. In virtually every case, I have checked the translation against the original Italian as Leonardo or his compiler wrote it in the manuscripts, which are available in facsimile editions, and I have adjusted the translations to reflect my own reading and interpretation of the original texts. In certain cases Leonardo's precepts and remarks have subtitles, some supplied by the compiler and others already given by Leonardo. Since they merely repeat the text of the statement, I have not included them.

The various statements were selected with their applicability to modern and contemporary art in mind, since I believe it can be demonstrated that much of Leonardo's theory of art, his advice to painters, and his remarks about art have the ring of enduring truth. Naturally I have loaded the dice to a certain extent by my selection of illustrations. Some have a nearly one-to-one relationship to the statements presented as their companions. Others have connections that are more oblique, occasionally tongue-in-cheek. Readers are encouraged to

---

*The Codex Atlanticus is a miscellaneous compilation of 401 folios of Leonardo's papers and drawings, not including the material from which Melzi compiled the *Treatise*, and is located in the Ambrosian Library, Milan.

make different connections than the ones I have selected; the choices are nearly infinite. Indeed, a selection of this sort must be somewhat idiosyncratic, and for that reason I have not sought an equal distribution between painters of one nation or another, one specific period or another. Widely known names are placed in company with lesser known painters without any formula.

The Introduction is followed by four chapters, each consisting of a cluster of statements by Leonardo and their appropriate illustrations preceded by a brief essay of my own concerning the material covered. While these remarks are not intended to invade the realm of Leonardo scholarship, I trust that in the context of this book they will bring to the reader new insights into Leonardo and his art.

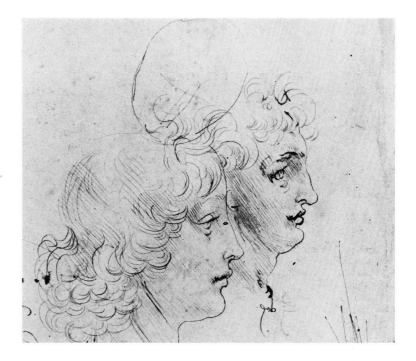

Introduction: Leonardo and Modern Art

Leonardo's fame has spread irregularly through the centuries, beginning in the first years following his apprenticeship in Florence during the mid-1470s. In assessing Leonardo's influence on the art that followed him, one should consider two types of material: (1) the actual contributions—his paintings, drawings, sculptures, and technical innovations; and (2) his ideas and precepts about painting as recorded in his own vast body of writings and as attributed to him in the writings of others. Both the work and the ideas have complex histories in which elements have been passed along, imitated, and commented upon at various times and in various places. Despite the intricacies of measuring such influence, we can safely say that Leonardo has been a constant factor in Western art through the centuries. In recent times there has been an increasing fascination with the historical Leonardo—as a genius and as a personality.

Leonardo was fortunate in learning the arts from a skilled and effective teacher—Andrea Verrocchio—who trained in his busy workshop a number of important painters besides Leonardo, including Lorenzo di Credi and probably Perugino and Ghirlandaio. What must have been particularly significant for Leonardo's formation in Verrocchio's *bottega* was the enormous range of activities conducted there, from the making of impressive altarpieces and panel pictures to large sculptural projects in marble and bronze to works in the "minor arts." Each of the more independent pupils took from Verrocchio what was most suitable to his individual development and vision. Leonardo makes this point when he advises the painter first to train his own hand by copying drawings of good masters under the guidance of his teacher, and then to represent objects well in relief [McM., no. 61]. Verrocchio's success as a molder of young artists is attested to by the fact that around 1500, as style and taste were undergoing impressive changes, Perugino and Leonardo

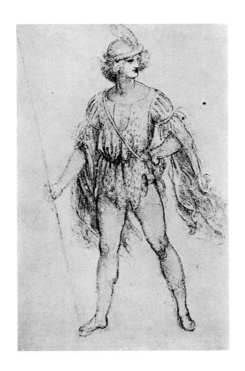

were considered the best painters in Italy (along with that remarkable representative of the older generation, Andrea Mantegna). Perugino, in turn, was the principal tutor of Pintoricchio and Raphael. Michelangelo had his first formal training as a painter under the highly successful if somewhat unimaginative Domenico Ghirlandaio. Thus through their teachers the three great innovators at the beginning of the sixteenth century—Leonardo, Michelangelo, and Raphael to a certain extent—were directly or indirectly indebted to Verrocchio's instruction. But however much these geniuses were influenced by their teachers, they were essentially on their own in the areas of invention and inspiration.

The teacher of a superior talent need not be particularly innovative or especially talented, but he should have absolute control over technique and be sympathetic to the requirements of his pupil. From circumstantial and documentary evidence, we can determine that Leonardo stayed with Verrocchio for as long as ten years, first presumably as a shop assistant and then as an independent master in the *bottega*. In fact, he remained with his master for at least four years after he had become a master in his own right in 1472.

The most noteworthy characteristic of Leonardo's early career, in light of his subsequent works, is its unspectacular and even undistinguished nature. Most of the works assigned to Leonardo during his years with Verrocchio, until at least 1476 and probably later—that is, until he was twenty-four or even twenty-six or twenty-seven—are rather uninspired Madonnas that follow closely the types and the sentiment developed within the workshop. Only with his unfinished *Adoration of the Magi* (Florence, Uffizi), a commission of 1481, does a fully independent and original artistic statement emerge. Michelangelo, on the other hand, made several masterpieces at a very early age, including the *Battle Relief*

(Florence, Casa Buonarroti) at about sixteen and the *Pietà* (Rome, St. Peter's), begun when he was twenty-two. And remember that Masaccio, a century earlier, had died in his twenty-eighth year and still managed to revolutionize the history of painting.

Leonardo's apparent dependence on Verrocchio for an extended period may reflect an unwillingness or even a fear to strike out on his own; the intimate relationship between the younger and the older master must have been difficult to break. It is surprising, however, to find not a single reference to Verrocchio in the hundreds of pages of Leonardo's notes. While Leonardo occasionally mentions other painters, he seems to have completely blocked out that connection. A serious falling out may have occurred at some point after 1476, when Leonardo is known to have been residing in Verrocchio's house. Perhaps a deep resentment of Verrocchio can be detected in Leonardo's advice about drawing a beautiful face:

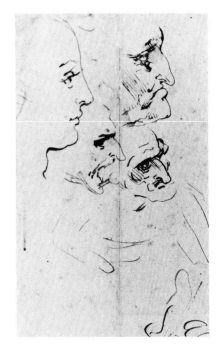

> ... *and if you were ugly, you would select faces that are not beautiful and you would paint ugly faces, as do many painters, whose painted figures often resemble that of their master.*
>
> [*McM.*, no. 276.]

Although he was himself the pupil of a distinguished artist, Leonardo never produced a pupil skilled enough or temperamentally (much less intellectually) suited to perpetuate his vision with any degree of fidelity; not one of his students became a first-rate painter. Great masters have not, as a rule, produced great pupils. The most extreme example is Michelangelo: among the handful of his assistants in painting, none achieved any degree of independent success or had, for that matter, real stature. Raphael is something of an exception because he did have a large number of young, highly talented *garzoni*, several of whom attained considerable fame. But during the lifetime of their master they were extensions of his ideas to such an extent that·it is often difficult to separate passages by Raphael from those by one or another assistant in his Roman workshop. Probably the most influential painter of modern times, Cézanne, who was indirectly at least the teacher and example for several generations of painters, had not a single student.

Leonardo did have pupils, close associates, and shop assistants at various times and he even shared an important commission, the *Madonna of the Rocks* (Paris, Louvre), with other masters. Perhaps the most gifted of his followers was Gian Antonio Boltraffio, but, on the whole, the list of those who mirrored the master's style consists of mostly mediocre painters. Their works hold interest for posterity primarily because they echo certain Leonardesque compositions and ideas that otherwise would have been lost.

In all justice to these painters, considering Leonardo's arsenal of ideas and skill, it would have been impossible for anyone to surpass or even make a significant achievement on Leonardo's own terms. Leonardo did not dedicate himself to painting assiduously, but carried on many varied activities so that the rhythm of his production and the training of his *garzoni* must have been erratic. Indeed, Leonardo was attacked by his contemporaries for his lack of perseverance as a painter. Such an irregular production could not have had a positive effect on his students.

Still, one cannot assume that Leonardo had no significant effect on his contemporaries simply because he had no outstanding close imitator. His art did have a determining impact on the pictorial language of Giorgione and Raphael, two of the finest painters of the generation

13

following Leonardo's. Raphael spent his earliest independent years in Florence, shortly after Leonardo had returned there from his extended stay in Milan, and following a brief period as military engineer and architect for Cesare Borgia. In Florence Raphael developed his famous series of Madonnas directly from Leonardesque ideas, modifying his innate sense of highly structured composition with Leonardo's innovations. And there is good reason to believe that Leonardo's example continued to serve Raphael for the rest of his life. The avenues by which Giorgione acquired Leonardo's lessons are more difficult to trace; Leonardo was in Venice for a few months in the winter of 1499–1500 and the two may have met there. But even if they did not, Giorgione shows knowledge of Leonardo's handling of light and shade and his *sfumato* ("smoky veil") technique, as Vasari recognized.

Did Leonardo have an influence on Michelangelo? The two are usually considered contemporaries, since their lives overlapped and incidents of hostility between them are recorded. But Leonardo was twenty-three years older than Michelangelo, and at the moment when Michelangelo was establishing his reputation in Florence with the marble *David*, Leonardo was returning home like a conquering hero, as the grand old man of painting. Hence it was Michelangelo who was competing with Leonardo and not vice versa. Despite the difference in their ages, the two artists shared Republican Florence's most prestigious pictorial commission, the mural decoration of the large assembly hall in the Palazzo Signoria (now called Palazzo Vecchio), where they were each to paint a battle scene, Leonardo the *Battle of Anghiari*, Michelangelo the *Battle of Cascina*. The cunning Florentine officials (including Machiavelli) probably felt they would obtain the best results with this double commission, since both masters would be unofficially competing for public approval. In any case, the project went ahead in promising fashion, and each artist invented new pictorial narratives of the highest order, but for different reasons neither master ever completed his work on the frescoes. Nevertheless, the cartoons that they prepared for eventual transfer onto the wall became the most treasured compositions of the sixteenth century. (They have not survived, but we know them through copies and engravings.) While there does not appear to be any direct influence of Leonardo on Michelangelo in the latter's battle scene, Michelangelo did make use of Leonardo's pictorial inventions for his *tondo* reliefs of the same years, and he made a rapid sketch of Leonardo's battle picture, as Raphael had done, representing, if not a sure sign of admiration, at least respect.

Leonardo's forms and images quickly spread throughout Italy and beyond the Alps during the first decades of the sixteenth century, largely by means of drawings and engravings. Albrecht Durer's knowledge of Leonardo's art helped to frame his Renaissance vocabulary and was instrumental in bringing Leonardo's artistic language to the North. Flanders seemed particularly ripe for certain of Leonardo's forms, and Quentin Massys, Jan Massys, Joos van Cleve, and Mabuse (Jan Gossaert) used Leonardesque elements while Leonardo was still alive, although it is not clear in each case how these forms reached the Lowlands. Interestingly, Leonardo was influenced by certain solutions of Netherlandish painters while developing his own sharply observed approach to nature.

Leonardo traveled a good deal during his lifetime. From Florence he went to Milan, Venice, Bologna, Mantua, back to Florence, then to Urbino and Piombino, and again to Milan, as well as to Pisa and Rome; and he spent his last years in France, where he died. He apparently took most of his paintings, drawings, scientific papers,

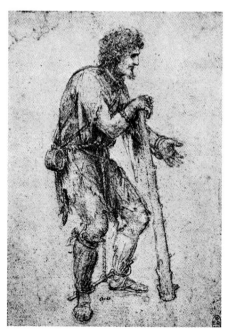

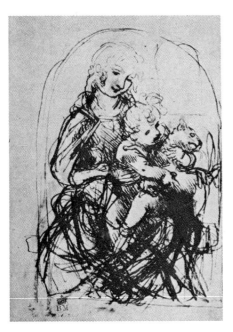

and notebooks on his travels, as well as a small entourage of servants and assistants. The effect of this habit was to spread the word wherever he went.

One can imagine the impression Leonardo must have made as an older man with a long white beard to go with his enormous learning, and a reputation for the bizarre. Vasari gives a hint of Leonardo's character in an account of how he constructed hollow wax animals that flew in the air when inflated and fell to the ground when the air escaped. He dipped lizards in quicksilver and fastened their scales to a live lizard, which trembled as it moved; after giving it eyes, a horn, and a beard, he tamed it. Vasari reports that everyone to whom Leonardo showed it ran away terrified. In one room in his Roman studio Leonardo kept a pair of bellows with which he would blow up the intestine of an animal until it filled the room, forcing everyone to seek safety in a corner. Leonardo himself describes one of his tricks thus:

> If you wish to make a fire which will set a large
> room ablaze without doing any harm you will
> proceed as follows: first perfume the air with dense
> fumes of incense or other strongly smelling thing,
> then boil and reduce to vapors ten pounds of
> brandy. But see that the room is closed tight, and
> throw powder of varnish among the fumes and
> this powder will be found floating upon the fumes;
> then seize a torch and enter suddenly into the
> room and instantly everything will become a sheet
> of flame.
>
> [MacC., p. 789.]

Whimsical experiments aside, Leonardo's diverse talents were evident early in his career. He was hired first as a musician in the Milanese court, according to Vasari, who tells us that Leonardo was an excellent extemporaneous rhymer. In a letter to the Duke of Milan, Ludovico

Sforza, known as Il Moro, Leonardo states that he is seeking employment and lists his expertise in a whole range of activities. In addition to painting, which is mentioned only parenthetically, Leonardo claims skill in marble, bronze, and terra-cotta sculpture—materials he must have learned how to deal with in Verrocchio's shop. He tells the duke that he is prepared to work on the gigantic equestrian statue of the duke's father, which had been planned for some time. Since Leonardo speaks of his ability in sculpture, it may be appropriate to remind the reader that he had a low opinion of sculpture in comparison with painting. Nevertheless, he was trained in carving and modeling and was regarded by his contemporaries as both a painter and a sculptor, as well as a goldsmith. In the letter, however, the principal skill that Leonardo emphasizes is his ability as a military engineer, an inventor of war machines of every type, and a builder of bridges. In times of peace, he adds, he is a capable architect of public and private buildings and canals (an important requirement at the time for the city of Milan and for Lombardy in general). The fields outlined in the letter are areas in which Leonardo worked during his lifetime, either in projects, drawings, or realized commissions.

Because this is such a famous letter, I cannot resist making a digression about its origin. As scholars know, the letter exists only in the form of a draft and it is not in Leonardo's own hand, but the assumption has always been made that the letter was sent and that it had the desired effect, namely, of obtaining employment in Milan. I believe that this is quite unlikely, if not impossible. At the time of the letter, around 1482 (although it is undated, internal and external evidence indicate that date), the Florentines and the Milanese were on good terms and it is unthinkable that the Duke of Milan would have hired a Florentine artist unknown to him unless he had been recommended by Lorenzo the Magnificent. And if there had been a recommendation by the head of the Florentine government, what would have been the point of such a letter? It would have been redundant. Furthermore, Leonardo—according to one early source—was closely connected with Lorenzo at this time, which makes it all the more likely that Lorenzo, as is usually assumed, arranged for Leonardo's employment in Milan.

I believe that the letter never reached a final draft and was never sent but was written as a kind of fantasizing on Leonardo's part. It nevertheless stands as an extraordinary document, especially considering the fact that when he composed (or dictated) it, much of the expertise he claimed for himself had never been tested. Yet in the years that followed, the activities listed became a reliable measure of Leonardo's interests. He was sought after and functioned as a military engineer and architect and even volunteered his services to the Venetians when they were menaced by the invading Turks; he was employed by Cesare Borgia in military campaigns to conquer parts of Umbria and the Marches, and he worked for the Florentine Signoria on an elaborate canalization project. These areas of specialization represent only a small part of the scope of Leonardo's mind. His drawings and notebooks cover material in the areas of philosophy, anatomy, physiology, natural history, medicine, optics, acoustics, astronomy, botany, geology, geography and topographical studies, flight, movement, weight, mathematics, the study of water and hydraulics, naval engineering, book collecting, and writing. All these pursuits lie outside the fine arts, yet the arts were the essence of his training and were at the core of his way of seeing and treating all the other categories. As a dedicated advocate of the importance of experience, Leonardo considered vision to be the most valuable sense; he regarded correct recording by means of painting and drawing as the highest achievement. Thus he was able to claim painting as

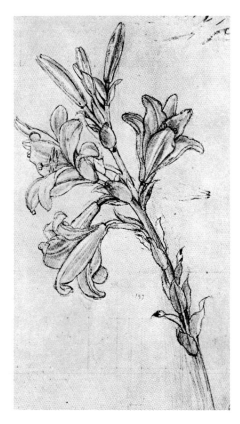

superior to the other arts, poetry and music as well as sculpture, and even superior to mathematics and geometry "because they are not concerned with quality, the beauty of nature's creations, and the harmony of the world."

Beyond his influence as a teacher and as an artistic personality, Leonardo exerted considerable influence on painters through his writings, the extent of which may be explained by his background. Leonardo came from a prosperous upper-middle-class family; his father, like many of his forebears, was a notary, a semiofficial occupation of considerable importance and trust. Leonardo was illegitimate, however, and by the rules of the guild to which the notaries belonged (*Arte de' Giudici e Notai*) he was not eligible to follow the profession. From the time he was a baby, therefore, he was destined for a craft or trade and his formal education in letters was not very intensive. Leonardo nevertheless had high regard for the power and importance of the written word. He accumulated an impressive personal library, the contents of which are known through lists in the Codex Atlanticus and in the recently discovered Madrid manuscripts. He collected books with great passion and his choices reflect the catholicity of his interests. Books on science and natural philosophy, herbal texts, agricultural treatises, and military handbooks formed part of his library; his concern with health, medicine, veterinary matters, and human and comparative anatomy were also reflected in his collection. In religious categories he owned books by the Church fathers, psalms, and, of course, a Bible. A selection of literary works both ancient and modern, and books on architecture, perspective, and optics, were also in his possession. Latin grammar books and vocabularies indicate that he taught himself Latin, which he had not studied as a child, and for that reason had regarded himself as a man without letters (*"omo sanza lettere"*).

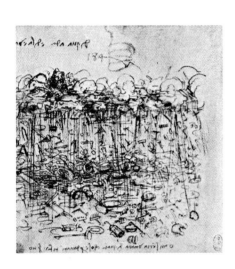

Leonardo intended to produce from his enormous body of notes (about half of which have survived) a number of books on various subjects, including flight, anatomy, and the dynamics of water, not to mention the treatise on painting, and perhaps others on architecture and sculpture, as scholars have recently suggested. Leonardo knew quite well that books could bring immortality, for his own library holdings were proof of the endurance of authors ancient and modern. At his death he left his manuscripts to Francesco Melzi as his most treasured possession.

Leonardo, who kept an intimate, detailed, and constant record of his thoughts, fantasies, inventions, and ideas, could hardly have been blind to the possibility that his words would be read. Far from being an attempt at secrecy, as is often assumed, his mirror writing was no barrier whatsoever to reading his manuscripts, for all one needs is a mirror. The best explanation for this extraordinary practice is that mirror writing is a natural method for a left-handed person (which Leonardo was) on whom the "normal" way is not imposed. That Leonardo was not discouraged from mirror writing as a child may be explained by the fact that he was ineligible to serve as a notary because of his illegitimate birth, and hence it did not make much difference to the family, who may even have thought the practice charming.

All of Leonardo's planned books have about them an unfinished quality, as do most of his paintings. Upon leaving Florence to work in Milan, he abandoned the *Adoration of the Magi*, his first majestic and highly innovative statement in art. The prestigious commission for the Palazzo Signoria depicting the *Battle of Anghiari* was advanced only to the cartoon state and work on the actual wall was interrupted because of a call to Milan, this time under French patronage. The pattern is true for easel pictures and portraits as well as for his sculptural commissions: the monumental Sforza equestrian statue and the Trivulzio tomb were never completed. As with Michelangelo, the *non-finito* master par excellence, one may find reasonable explanations for Leonardo's inability to finish one or another particular work: political conditions were often unstable, patrons died or lost favor with the ruling powers, governments changed. Still, if Leonardo is compared to contemporaries of equal stature like Raphael and Titian, he is seen as a hardened procrastinator. Vasari severely criticized his inability to complete works and illustrated this with the following anecdote: Having been commissioned to do a work for Pope Leo X (Giovanni de' Medici), Leonardo—by that time rather old—immediately went ahead to prepare the oil and herbs for making the varnish. This circumstance prompted the Pope to exclaim, "Heavens, he is good for nothing because he begins to think about the end before beginning to work."

In some cases where work had proceeded more systematically, the seeds of disintegration seemed built in by the master himself. The *Last Supper*, probably the most famous mural ever painted, started decaying soon after it was finished, if in fact it *was* finished, since it is said that Leonardo could not complete the face of Christ. Leonardo never completed his literary efforts either; not a single manuscript was prepared in final form for publication, nor was anything printed during Leonardo's lifetime; the enormous body of writing and plans for books on a variety of subjects remained in a state of *non-finito*.

Perhaps Leonardo's reluctance to begin an undertaking and to complete those begun can be clarified by one of his own remarks:

> When one's work is equal to one's judgment, that
> is a bad sign for one's judgment; and when one's
> work surpasses one's judgment that is worse, as
> happens to the painter who is amazed at having

done so well; and when judgment exceeds the
work, that is a very good sign and if he is young
and of such disposition, without doubt he will be
an excellent artist. If he composes few works, they
will be of such quality as to make men stop and
contemplate their perfection with admiration.
[*McM., no.* 439.]

Since the nineteenth century Leonardo da Vinci has occupied a unique position in Western cultural life on at least three levels, as mythic figure, artist, and writer. Leonardo represents the universal man, indeed the most universal of universal men, the genius who worked in a score of different areas, a great inventor and innovator. Once the airplane became an everyday reality, Leonardo's efforts as a Renaissance Daedalus became the common knowledge of every schoolboy, and modern scientific historians have even found the prototype of the helicopter in Leonardo's drawings.

Several of Leonardo's paintings have become well-known images on almost every cultural level in modern society. The *Mona Lisa* and the *Last Supper* are probably the best known pictures of all time. The wide recognition and adulation of Leonardo and his works by the public is paralleled by a similar admiration by painters, especially during the past hundred years, although on different terms and for different reasons. Artists are engaged by his poetic, veiled atmosphere, his softened forms, the clarity of his narrative, the beauty and spontaneity of his drawings, his absolute control of the human figure and its anatomy, his use of several kinds of perspective, the romance of his landscapes. Admiration produced direct borrowings as well as a more generalized influence. The *Mona Lisa* has been both the butt of artistic jokes and the object of imitation; the composition of the *Last Supper* has been used by filmmakers who have recog-

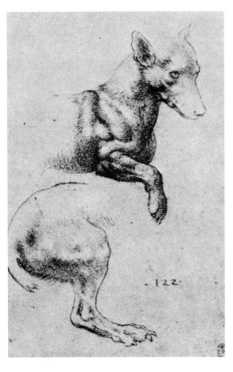

. 122 .

nized the complexity of the psychological interaction of the personalities found in the painting.

The influence of Leonardo's pictures and his figure compositions can be recognized rather easily in the work of various artists. Salvador Dali, Fernand Léger, Pavel Tchelitchew, Kasimir Malevich, Andy Warhol, Marcel Duchamp, Odilon Redon, James Brooks, and Jasper Johns among others have made overt references to Leonardo. Less easy to ascertain in terms of direct influence on form-making and visual habits are Leonardo's ideas about art, the subject that occupies the remainder of this book. Before entering into that question, however, a word must be said about Leonardo's own sources—the influences on him. Just as in his paintings we can trace elements of his teacher, Verrocchio, certain non-Florentine Italian painters such as Antonello da Messina and Andrea Mantegna, a few Northern European masters, and artists of Classical antiquity, so we can find in his writings about art and his ideas about painting a traditional quotient. His intellectual sources were of two kinds, those emanating from the ancient world, and those from the cultural ambiance of his immediate predecessors, especially among the Florentines.

Ancient writers, particularly Pliny, who wrote the most complete surviving pages about the arts in Greco-Roman times, had a direct impact on Leonardo, but classical ideas were transmitted to him indirectly as well, through the works of earlier fifteenth-century writers who themselves had borrowed ideas and concepts from antiquity. Among the fifteenth-century writers who should be mentioned is Cennino Cennini, a minor painter whose handbook on painting reflected the prevalent points of view before the vigorous changes of the early Renaissance. The sculptor and goldsmith Lorenzo Ghiberti, whose principal works include two sets of bronze doors for the Florentine Baptistry, wrote influen-

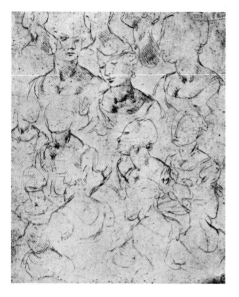

tial pages on art both ancient and modern in his *Commentarii*, which Leonardo apparently knew. The treatises of the Florentine Antonio Filarete and the Sienese Francesco di Giorgio, both architects interested in all the arts, were also familiar to Leonardo, and we know that he owned and annotated a manuscript by Francesco di Giorgio. It may also be assumed that Leonardo was familiar with Piero della Francesca's writings on perspective and mathematics since he was on very friendly terms with Piero's countryman and follower Luca Pacioli.

Probably the most important single influence on Leonardo's thought was Leon Battista Alberti, the most influential writer on the arts in Italy during the fifteenth century. Born into an aristocratic Florentine family that had been exiled, Alberti was permitted to return to the city in the late 1420s and soon afterward wrote the fundamental work *On Painting*, in both Italian and Latin, and dedicated it to the leading artists of the early Renaissance. Alberti also wrote an immensely influential book on architecture, and another on sculpture. He claimed to have painted and sculpted, although his experience must have been quite limited and his works amateurish. Even in the case of architecture, though several highly influential buildings of the period are assigned to him—the façade of Santa Maria Novella in Florence, the Rucellai Palace in the same city, important churches in Rimini and Mantua—his precise role is not easily determined. Alberti was essentially an intellectual, a humanist who wrote plays in Latin in the Roman fashion, tracts on a number of literary subjects, and a book on the family; he was only incidentally an architect. Still, since his interests cover so many fields, he has been justifiably considered, like Leonardo da Vinci and Francesco di Giorgio, one of the universal men representing the highest accomplishments of the Renaissance.

An artist trained in a workshop, unlike Alberti,

who was educated in the university, Leonardo developed a determined and unwavering reliance upon the truth of experience. As we have seen, Leonardo had an extensive personal library and was aware of the history of ideas as they came down to him. But even when he borrowed directly, Leonardo consistently tested the ideas within the context of the laboratory, that is, by his own experience in the studio.

At a time when painters were only beginning to shake themselves loose from the artisan class, from the mechanical arts and the shopkeeper category, Leonardo regarded painting as one of the most significant human activities. In fact, his favorable estimation of painting is so unqualified that it must produce pride and self-confidence in those painters who read his statements on the subject. Why he came to hold painting in such high esteem may be discovered, at least in part, in the story of his childhood. As Leonardo developed his skill in painting and widened his intellectual interests, he may have wished to increase the significance of his activity by placing it above all others, including not only sculpture, its natural parallel, but also music and poetry. He must have evaluated it above the notary's art, from which he was excluded because of his illegitimate birth. We can also imagine that Leonardo later developed this point in reaction to the humanists who surrounded the Medici family; although he seems to have been connected peripherally with the Medici, he was never sympathetic to the humanists. And we know that Lorenzo the Magnificent was a poet not overly devoted to painting.

The comparison between painting and the other arts is at the heart of what has come to be known as Leonardo's "Paragone" (Comparison), which forms an important section of his *Treatise on Painting*. The discussion probably reflects an actual dispute among the artists of the time and perhaps among the humanists, who

25

would surely have looked unfavorably on Leonardo's opinions. The argument in various forms continued with considerable vigor well into the sixteenth century when the comparison centered on the relative merits of painting and sculpture. As an old man, however, Michelangelo seemed bored by the question; he was, after all, an expert in both areas (as was Leonardo, for that matter). Ever since the Renaissance the practice of ranking the different arts has continued, although in recent years the boundaries between sculpture, painting, and architecture have blurred considerably. The primacy of painting in Leonardo's mind had to do with the primacy of sight among the senses; he advocated the superiority of visual illustration over verbal description. He rejected the famous statement of Horace *"Ut pictura poesis"* (as is painting, so is poetry), in favor of painting. In fact, Leonardo retorts:

> *If you [poets] call painting silent poetry,*
> *then the painter may say that poetry is*
> *blind painting.*
>
> [*McM., no. 30.*]

In developing his ideas about painting, Leonardo was keenly aware of his immediate predecessors—the generation represented by Masaccio, Donatello, and Brunelleschi— and of ancient writers, although he rarely uses a reverent tone in discussing the Greco-Roman world. In declaring that:

> *the first picture was nothing but the outline*
> *that surrounds the shadow of a man made*
> *by the sun on walls*
>
> [*McM., no. 98.*]

Leonardo was essentially repeating an ancient notion

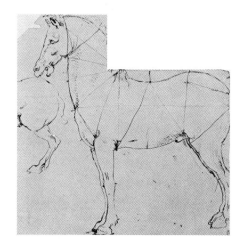

that had already been cited by Alberti and Ghiberti. The idea is also found in Pliny the Elder and Quintilian, whom Alberti credits with the observation.

The power of the painted subject to fool the eye (and mind) of the viewer was also part of Leonardo's theory of art, and he recounts that:

> *Paintings even deceive animals, for I have*
> *seen a picture that deceived a dog because*
> *of the likeness to its master; likewise I have*
> *seen dogs bark and try to bite painted*
> *dogs, and a monkey that did an infinite*
> *number of foolish things with another painted*
> *monkey. I have seen flying swallows light*
> *on painted iron bars before the windows*
> *of buildings.*
>
> [*McM., no. 31.*]

The mystical properties of painted images did not escape Leonardo. In the "Paragone" he points out that:

> *By means of painting, lovers are impelled*
> *towards the portraits of the beloved, and*
> *speak to the paintings that portray the*
> *appearance of the beloved; by it the people*
> *are moved to beseech portraits of the gods*
> *making fervent vows: [but] this is not*
> *brought about by looking at the works of*
> *poets, who represent the same gods*
> *with words.*
>
> [*McM., no. 31.*]

The unique quality of painting, its originality and its inimitable character, made Leonardo its most eloquent defender. On the subject the following words are among the most moving ever written:

It [painting] cannot be taught to those who are not naturally fitted for it, as can mathematics, where the disciple absorbs as much as the teacher reads to him. It cannot be copied as can letters, where the copy is worth as much as the original. It cannot be cast, as sculpture can, where the cast is worth as much as the original, insofar as the excellence of the work is concerned. It does not have an infinity of progeny as do printed books. Painting alone remains noble, it alone brings honor to its author and remains precious and unique, never bringing forth children equal to itself. . . .

[McM., no. 18.]

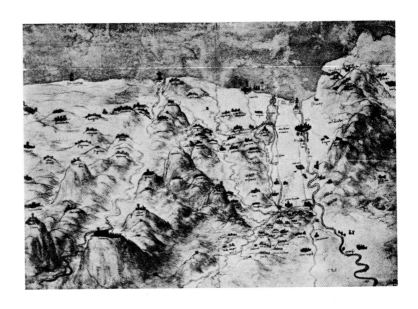

I. Creative Invention: The Painter and Painting

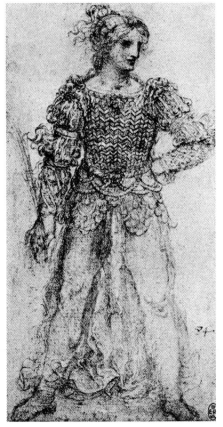

Leonardo comes particularly close to contemporary thinking and practice in the area of pictorial invention. During his waking hours and probably during sleep—at least while lying in bed—Leonardo was constantly thinking. He was obsessed with the economical use of time and seemed to live by certain aphorisms common in Tuscany, such as "A life well spent is long." He jotted this line down in one of the notebooks along with a variation, "As a well-spent day brings happy sleep, so life well used brings happy death." Leonardo never treated the imagery of his paintings in a common or habitual way; through constant study and interpretation his active mind was continually revising a given subject.

Leonardo criticized his friend Sandro Botticelli for not giving proper attention to the landscapes in his paintings by failing to finish the details. According to Leonardo, Botticelli claimed that the mere throwing of a sponge full of diverse colors at a wall could leave a stain in which a fine landscape might occur. Such a notion could have been obtained from antiquity: Pliny tells of the Greek painter Protogenes having difficulty painting the froth on a dog's mouth. He painted and repainted the area until finally in disgust he threw the sponge that he had used to clean the picture at the crucial spot. And behold, the froth was perfect. Leonardo saw the matter rather differently from Botticelli and the ancients; he emphasized the potentialities of invention on the part of the painter who observed such a stain, not the happy accident that left a perfect element in the painting. The general notion of seeking forms and ideas in accidental situations is repeated in several places in Leonardo's writings. He "discovered" for himself a process to stimulate the imagination during his adult life and he described it in his *Treatise* for the benefit of other painters. He advised the painter to look at the stains on a wall and find heads of men, diverse animals, battles, rocks, seas, clouds, woods, and other things, and he noted how like this is to the sound of bells, in which one hears what one likes. You may find, he said, the same things by looking at stones of various colors, the ashes of a fire, clouds, or mud.

A younger contemporary of Leonardo in Florence, Piero di Cosimo (1462–1521), is usually considered one of the most eccentric artistic personalities of the period. Vasari recounts how Piero would stop to study a wall where sick persons habitually spat. There he would evisage battles of horses, fantastic cities, and enormous landscapes; he did the same when looking at clouds. It is probable that Piero knew of Leonardo's recommendations since he was an admirer of Leonardo's art.

It is very likely that Leonardo actually used this technique in developing compositions. The fantastical landscapes in the *Mona Lisa* and the *Madonna of the Rocks* may have derived from this process and so may certain drawings in which the forms seem to have been pulled out of a maze of light and shadow to establish the composition. This process is exactly opposite to the traditional method of having the final compositional entity in mind from the start, as in Michelangelo's approach to marble where the idea of a work is first fixed in the mind of the artist who then carves away the excess material to reveal or release the figure from its stone prison.

The objects or phenomena that Leonardo urges the painter to contemplate—stained walls, colored stones, clouds, mud, ashes—are composed of light and shade and are devoid of hard edges or sharp lines. Thus they can be manipulated in the artist's imagination almost at will.

Closely connected with his ideas concerning invention and imagination are those about the working conditions of artists for the relationship between environment and productivity is obvious and of primary importance to every artist. A perplexing choice faces the painter: to work alone, undisturbed by social interaction, or to paint and draw with others. The answer for a twentieth-century artist probably rests on two prime considerations; first, the temperament of the individual and whether he can effectively produce while others are around him; and second, the artist's financial situation.

Leonardo was aware of these issues, and his own attitude was ambivalent, as we see in the varying statements he made in his writings. At one point Leonardo maintains that it is better to work in company, for several reasons. Competition, a *sine qua non* in his native Florentine tradition, will spur the artist on to better work, he says. Furthermore, a painter can learn from those less skilled, since he will recognize and reject their errors. But given free choice, Leonardo says he would elect to work alone, for "If you are alone, you belong entirely to yourself; if you are accompanied by even one companion, you belong only half to yourself." What prevented him from withdrawing from society, it seems, is that in so doing he would have been looked upon as mad. He seems to have feared public castigation, and in a revealing passage he writes that he fears loneliness as well. Elsewhere he advises that "a painter's companions should resemble him in his interests, and if he fails to find any such, he should accustom himself to be alone in his investigations, for in the end he will find no more profitable companionship."

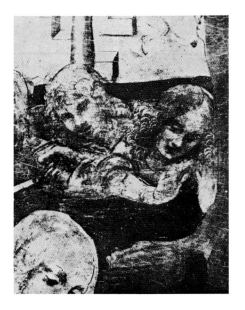

Leonardo also remarks that an artist when painting ought not to refuse to hear anyone's opinion, for "we know very well that though a man may not be a painter, he may have a true conception of the form of another man." Leonardo advises painters to "be desirous of hearing patiently the opinion of others, and consider and reflect carefully whether or not he who censures you has reason for his censure." Such an open attitude toward an evaluation of his work is unexpected, but there is reason to believe that Leonardo actually conducted himself as he advised. During the painting of the *Last Supper* visitors came frequently and their opinions were solicited and presumably considered seriously by the artist—a far cry from Michelangelo's highly secretive practice while painting the Sistine Ceiling. Leonardo's advice was not new. The notion that a painter should listen to everyone, reflect upon the matter for himself, and then make the necessary emendations had already been set down in the fifteenth century by Alberti in *On Painting*, from which Leonardo may have taken the idea. Alberti himself was dependent upon ancient authors for this point: Pliny the Elder reports a similar practice in his discussion of Apelles, who is said to have been the greatest painter of antiquity, although nothing has survived of his art.

Leonardo was also much concerned with self-criticism and self-analysis of works by painters and some of his observations are particularly pertinent even in the contemporary situation. He asserts:

> *We know well that errors are more easily recognized in the works of others than in one's own, so that often while criticizing the small errors of others you will overlook your own great faults. . . . I say that when you are painting you should take a flat mirror and often look at your work in it, and it will then be seen in reverse, and will appear to be by the hand of some other master, and you will be better able to judge its errors than in any other way.*

> *It is also good every now and then to go away and have a little relaxation; for then when you come back to the work your judgment will be better, since to remain constantly at work causes you to deceive yourself.*

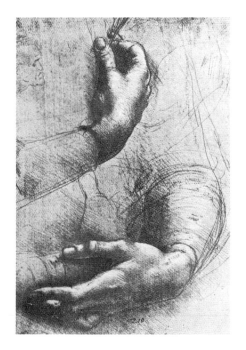

It is also good to move some distance away, because then the work appears smaller, and besides it is taken in at a glance, and a lack of harmony and proportion in the various parts and in the colors is better recognized than it is up close.
[*McM., no. 440.*]

In the "Paragone" Leonardo gives an ideal description of the painter at work. Comfortably dressed, the painter holds light brushes (as opposed to the heavy tools of the sculptor) and sits in front of his work, upon which he has placed attractive colors. The painter's house, full of fine paintings, is clean, unlike that of the sculptor. The air is filled with music or the sounds of poetry read aloud, without the interference of pounding hammers as in a sculptor's studio. Leonardo's deprecation of the sculptor as merely a worker with his hands, a craftsman, echoes ideas about the status of the sculptor found in Plutarch and Lucian. No music or poetic readings could have entertained Michelangelo during the extreme discomfort and physical strain of his work on the tomb for Julius II, for example. Leonardo's routine, however, on a typical day in Milan would involve painting on the *Last Supper* in Santa Maria della Grazia, then going to work on the model of the colossal horse in the Sforza Palace, then attending to duties at the court, always accompanied by a small retinue of assistants.

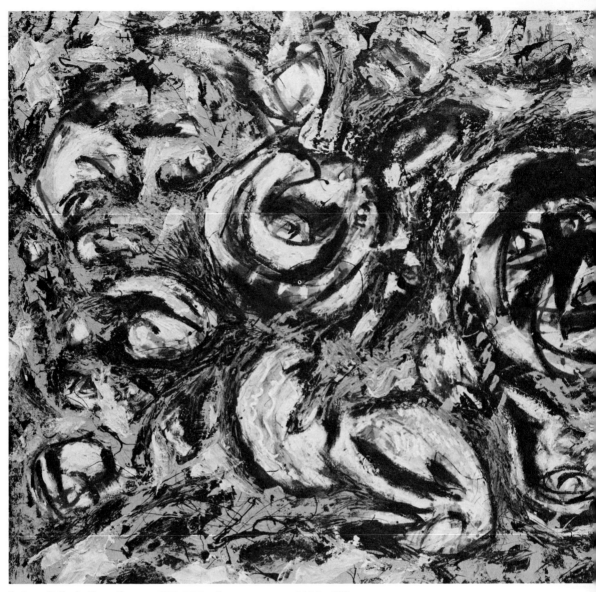

Jackson Pollock, *Ocean Grayness 1953*, 1953, oil on canvas, cm. 146.5 x 229.

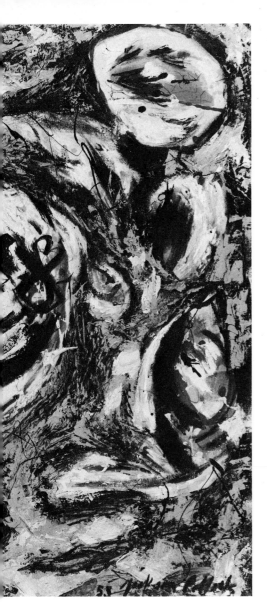

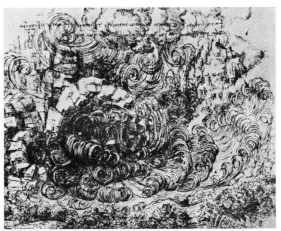

Look at certain walls dirtied with various stains
or with a mixture of different kinds of stones. If
you have to invent some scene you will be able to
see in them a resemblance to various landscapes
adorned with mountains, rivers, rocks, trees,
plains, wide valleys and hills. You will also be
able to see various battles and figures in quick
movements, and strange expressions on faces, and
costumes, and an infinite number of things which
you can then reduce into separate, well-conceived
form. With such walls and mixtures of different
stones the same thing happens as it does with the
sound of bells, in whose pealing you may discover
every name and word that you can imagine.
[McM., no. 76 and cf.
no. 93.]

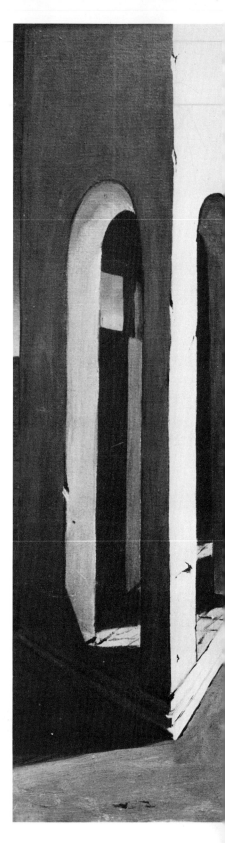

*The divine provides that the mind of the painter
in the science of painting transmute itself into a
likeness of the divine mind. With free power it
reasons concerning the generation of the diverse
natures of the various animals, plants, fruits,
landscapes, fields, ruins in the mountains, fearful
and frightful places which bring terror to those
who view them, and also pleasant places, soft and
delightful with flowery meadows in various colors,
swayed by the soft waves of breezes, looking beyond the wind that escapes from them, rivers that
descend from the high mountains with the impetus
of great floods, dragging along uprooted trees
mixed with stones, roots, earth and foam, carrying away everything that opposes it to ruin. And
so too the sea with its storms. . . .*

[McM., no. 280.]

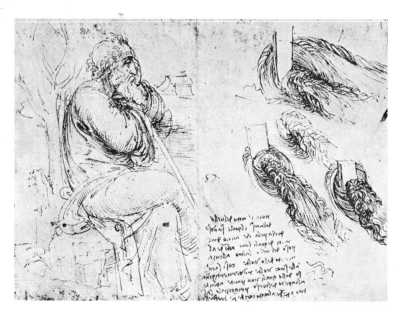

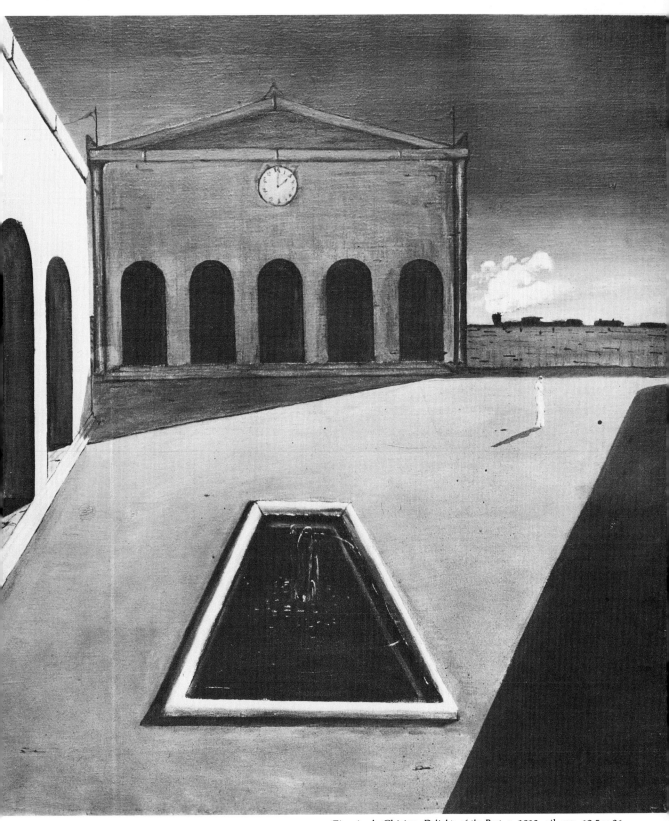

Giorgio de Chirico, *Delights of the Poet*, c. 1913, oil, cm. 69.5 x 86.

Frederick Edwin Church, *Morning in the Tropics*, 1877, oil on canvas, cm. 138 x 213.5.

The air, as soon as it is light, is filled with innu-
merable images to which the eye serves as a
magnet.

[*MacC.*, *p.* 63 *and cf.*
p. 994.]

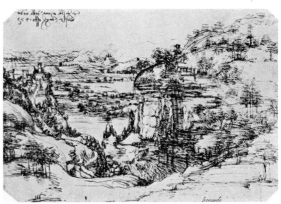

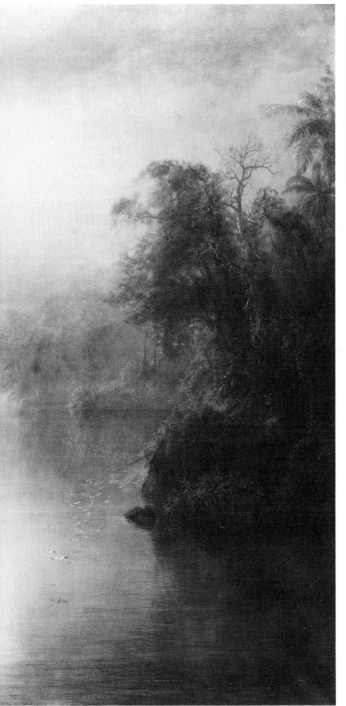

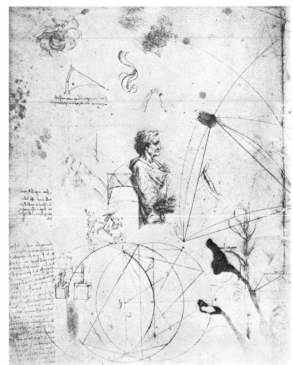

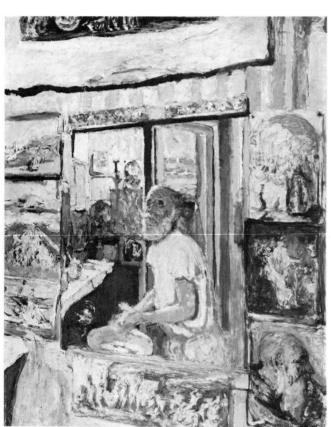

Edouard Vuillard,
Self-portrait of the Artist in His Studio,
1923, oil, cm. 63.5 x 81.

So that the well-being of the body may not ruin
that of the mind, the painter or draughtsman
ought to be solitary, especially when he is intent
on those reflections and considerations that, by
being continually present before his eyes, furnish
food to be stored up in the memory. If you are
alone, you belong entirely to yourself; if you are
accompanied by even one companion, you belong
only half to yourself, and that much less in proportion to the thoughtlessness of his conduct; and
if you have more than one companion, you will
fall more deeply into the same plight. If you
should say, I will do things my own way; I will
draw apart, so that I may be the better able to reflect the forms of natural objects, then I say this
system must turn out badly, for you will not be
able to prevent yourself from often lending an ear
to their chatter; and since it is impossible to serve
two masters you will discharge badly the role of
companion, and even worse, that of reflecting on
art. And if you say, I will withdraw so far apart
that their words will not reach me nor in any
way disturb me, to you I reply that in this case
you will be looked upon as crazy, and bear in
mind that in so doing, you would also be alone.

[McM., no. 74.]

I say and affirm that it is much better for many reasons to draw in company than alone. First, you will be ashamed of yourself to be seen among the group of men drawing inadequately and this mortification will be a motive for studying well. Secondly, a sound envy will stimulate you to become among those more praised than yourself, and the praise of others will spur you on. Another reason is that you will learn something from the way in which those who are better than you draw. If you are better than others, you will benefit by despising their defects, while the praise of others will increase your skill.

[*McM., no. 73.*]

Pablo Picasso, *Intérieur au les Menines*, oil.

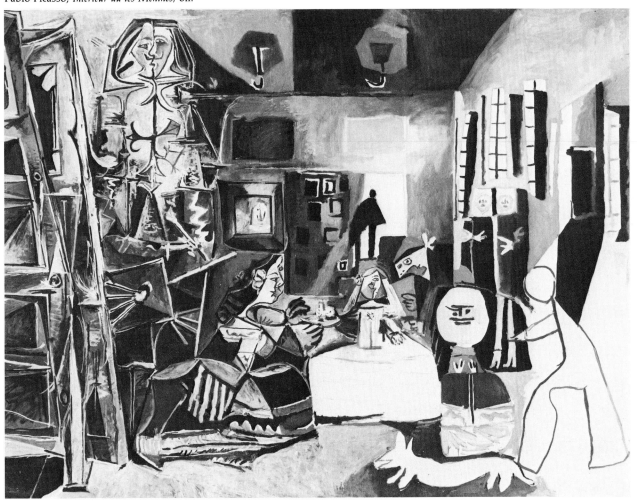

II. The Figure and Expression

The rendering of the human figure was a central topic of Leonardo's artistic theories. During the late 1460s and early 1470s, when he was training, the main workshops in Florence were deeply involved in the realistic and detailed interpretation of the human body. Artists like Verrocchio and Antonio and Piero Pollaiuolo—all of whom were engaged in sculpture as well as painting—began the rigorous tradition of figure studies that remains a vital part of art instruction today. Leonardo, who had greater control over anatomy than any artist before him and most who followed him, is more functional than theoretical when directing his advice concerning anatomy to painters. While he believes that a painter should know the mechanics of the human body in motion, he warns painters not to exaggerate the muscles and tendons lest the result be a figure that looks like a "sack full of walnuts" or a "bundle of radishes," descriptions that are among the most picturesque in his writings. Such remarks, repeated several times in the notebooks, have usually been interpreted as an attack on Michelangelo's treatment of the figure, giving further fuel to the legend of heated competition between the two giants. Actually, the charge that their nudes look like sacks of walnuts is more appropriately applied to certain Michelangelesque imitators and interpreters who postdate Leonardo's remark by decades than to Michelangelo himself. I suspect that Leonardo had in mind the art of his teachers and of their generation; in their enthusiastic "discovery" of muscles and bones, the Pollaiuolo brothers and Verrocchio did make unbelievable wooden figures, although the sculpted nudes of Baccio Bandinelli, court favorite of the sixteenth-century Medici, certainly offer striking examples of what Leonardo had disparaged.

Leonardo himself, with all his knowledge, never fell into the trap of showing off his mastery of anatomy. His skill with anatomical parts was a tool for rendering

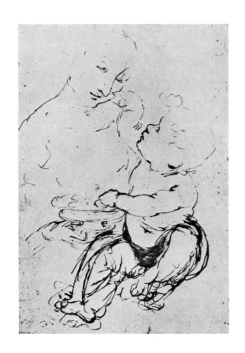

the figure as a whole, not an end in itself. Nor was he unaware of the strong personal elements that can enter into rendering the figure. He warns that the painter who had ugly hands may reproduce them in the figures of his paintings; such is also true with the other parts of the body. Consequently he advises painters:

> Take careful note of that part of yourself
> which is most ugly and correct it in your
> work. For if you are like a beast your
> figures will be the same and devoid of
> talent and in like manner every part of the
> body, good or bad, that you have within
> you will be in part revealed in your figures.
> [McM., no. 85.]

Leonardo's advice regarding the actual method of drawing or painting the human body seems to have been followed by later figure painters. The entire figure should be sketched in, even if very summarily, before individual parts are worked up: otherwise the result might appear to be inorganic and the unity of the whole be endangered. Most painters do this naturally, but, judging from extant drawings, we may assume that such an instinct did not rule before Leonardo's time. Sculpture offers an analogous situation. When a sculpted figure is destined for a niche or a position against a wall, the back is not intended to be seen, and parts that will be hidden from view once the statue is installed need not be modeled. Yet Renaissance sculptors usually worked out these areas, as did the carvers of the Parthenon's pediments. In order to give conviction to the exposed parts, the artist has to maintain control of the entire figure.

Leonardo specifically refers to the use of *contrapposto* in rendering the figure; that is, an arrangement of the figure so that the weight is distributed unequally from one side to the other and so that the various parts of the body, the shoulders, hips, knees, are on different levels on each side of the body. He does not, however, refer to ancient practice, where this system of distributing the limbs and weights in the body was first employed. Leonardo's motive for advocating *contrapposto* lies in the search for variety, movement, and interest. Simply speaking, he observed:

> *When a man or other creature moves either*
> *rapidly or slowly, that side which is above*
> *the leg that supports the body will always*
> *be lower than the opposite side.*
> [*McM., no. 347.*]

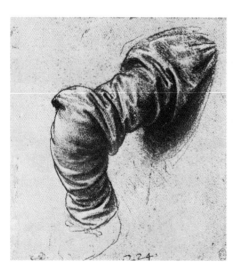

Here he was following once again the established practice of his Florentine predecessors, although Leonardo was a considerable innovator in the use of *contrapposto*, especially in portraiture, where he broke away from the static frontal or pure-profile representations common to that genre.

One of Leonardo's exercises was to isolate all the possible positions of the human figure that can be rendered by the painter, or at least those that should be recognized and understood by the painter. In doing so, he based his judgment on empirical evidence, as was his practice, seeking to establish common-sense ground rules and definitions. There is considerable repetition in Leonardo's notes, as he himself realized, and this is particularly the case when he speaks about movement. Nevertheless, his arguments vary according to his objectives in different sections, and his views about movement are by no means consistent. Although concerned with a wide range of figure poses, he explored very few of the possibilities in his own paintings. His younger contemporaries (Michelangelo and, to a lesser extent, Raphael) appear to have been fascinated by the potentialities of a range of movements and poses. Michelangelo's Sistine Ceiling frescoes probably offer the best examples in the period. In fact, in the fresco of the *Flood* we see illustrated in a single narrative scene practically all of Leonardo's eighteen identified positions which he gives as:

> *To be still, to move, to run, to be upright, to be*
> *supported, to sit, to bend over, to kneel, to lie*
> *down, to be suspended, to carry, to be carried, to*
> *push, to pull, to strike, to be struck, to make*
> *heavy, to raise up.*
>
> [McM., no 374.]

Raphael in his Vatican *Stanze* frescoes also worked out a large number of positions, and we know that Leonardo had at least an indirect role in the development of Raphael's artistic language.

The problem of poses has always been a central concern for figure painters. When rendering from the model, that is, when drawing from life, the question of poses is also critical because the painter instructs his model to take the poses that interest him. These are based on visual experience from nature to be sure, but also upon the images the artist has experienced from the pictorial heritage in which he operates. He may thus place his model in attitudes derived ultimately from antiquity or from Renaissance and Baroque types without necessarily realizing it. Perhaps a particularly challenging aspect of the question is the rate of speed with which a particular movement is undertaken. If such was not a pressing issue for Renaissance artists, it has engaged and challenged modern masters and has become, for some, the principal theme of their art.

As is frequently the case in the development of Leonardo's ideas, the Greco-Roman tradition lies beneath more direct impulses from his Renaissance predecessors, but regardless of source the ideas were habitually tested and confirmed by Leonardo's own experience. This situation is particularly relevant for his concept of "decorum," or appropriateness, one of the most pervasive aesthetic concepts of late antique poetics and rhetoric. Leonardo adapted preexisting concepts for his own purposes. He advocated a clarity and directness of gesture and movement that became one of the characteristic features of all later Renaissance painting from Raphael to Titian, and since then from Poussin to David. The *Last Supper* can serve as an illustration of "decorum" in spite of its poor condition. This is one case in which Leonardo's theory and practice came into harmony. While Leonardo's intention has sometimes been regarded as highly ambiguous and multileveled, particularly in the *Mona Lisa* and the *Last Supper*, his objectives seen within the boundaries of his art theory lead to the opposite conclusion, namely, that the meanings are straightforward.

Leonardo was concerned with representing the totality of figures, not merely with an outward appearance. Ghirlandaio painted several Last Suppers of considerable artistic worth but his actors lack inner life and motivation for their actions; the results are hollow. Leonardo, on the other hand, sought to express "the intent of the mind" of his subjects, admittedly a difficult task. His writings on this point include the following passage:

> *A picture or rather painted figures ought to be done in such a way that those who see them may be able with ease to recognize from their attitudes what is passing through their minds. So if you have to represent a man of good repute in the act of speaking, make his gestures accord with the probity of his speech; and similarly if you have to*

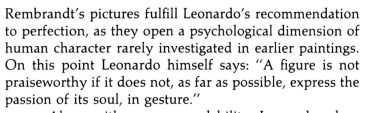

represent a brutal man, make him with fierce movements flinging out his arms towards his hearer, and the head and chest protruding forward beyond the feet should seem to accompany the hands of the speaker.

Just so a deaf mute who sees two people talking, although himself deprived of the power of hearing, is none the less able to understand from the movements and features of the speakers the subject of their discussion.

[*MacC. p. 902.*]

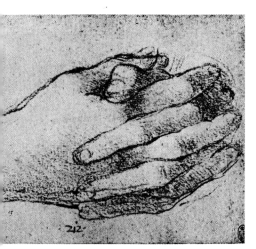

Rembrandt's pictures fulfill Leonardo's recommendation to perfection, as they open a psychological dimension of human character rarely investigated in earlier paintings. On this point Leonardo himself says: "A figure is not praiseworthy if it does not, as far as possible, express the passion of its soul, in gesture."

Along with an easy readability, Leonardo advocates a harmony within each figure so that the age, sex, and station are consistent with the individual represented. This harmony should be achieved not only by a representation of anatomy and by the proportions of the figure but also by the depiction of the figure's attire. In a characteristically insightful passage, Leonardo warns painters to be careful not to impose their own features on personages in their pictures, perhaps in response to an observation attributed to Cosimo de' Medici that "every painter paints himself."

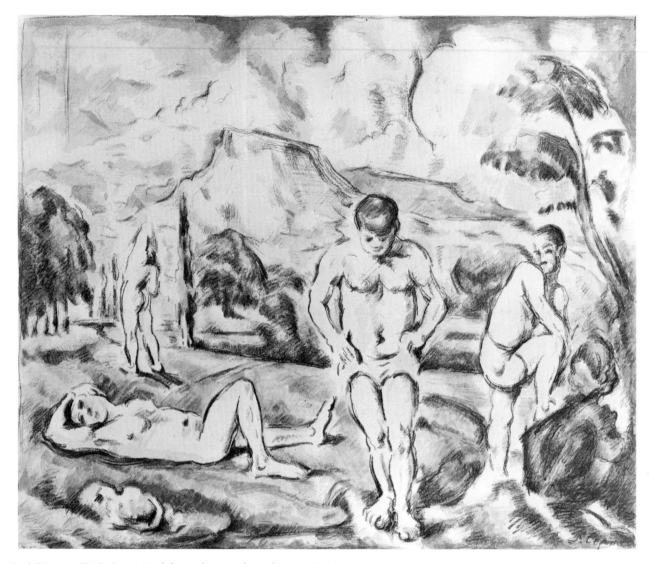

Paul Cézanne, *The Bathers*, 1899, lithograph, printed in color, cm. 42.5 x 52.

It is a necessary thing for the painter, in order to be good at arranging parts of the body in attitudes and gestures which can be represented in the nude, to know the anatomy of the nerves, bones, muscles, and tendons. He should know their various movements and forces, and which nerve or muscle occasions each movement, and paint those only distinct and enlarged and not the others, as do many who, in order to appear to be great draughtsmen, make their nudes wooden and without grace, so that they seem more like a sack full of walnuts than the surface of a human being, or indeed, a bundle of radishes rather than muscular nudes.

[McM., no. 329.]

Do not make all the muscles of your figures evident because when they are in their place they are not in great evidence, if the members over which they are situated are not in strong action or activity. The members that are at rest are without a show of muscles. And if you do otherwise, you have imitated more a sack of walnuts than a human figure.

[Madrid II, fol. 128r.]

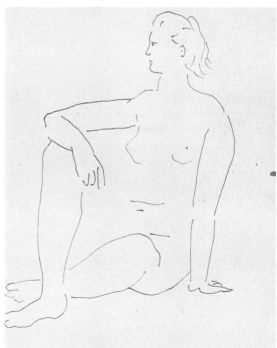

Pablo Picasso, *Femme Assise*, ink on paper.

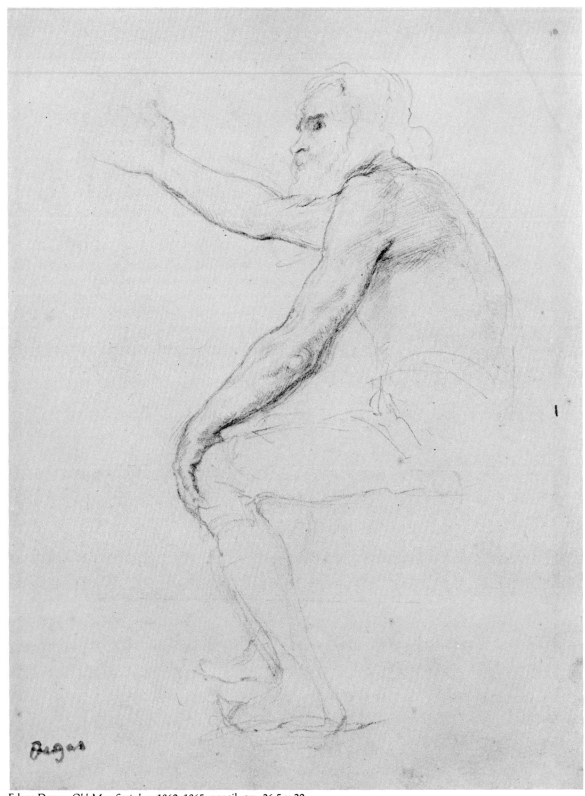

Edgar Degas, *Old Man Seated*, c. 1860–1865, pencil, cm. 26.5 x 20.

When you draw nudes be careful always to draw the whole figure, and then finish that part which seems to you the best and then work that part in with the other parts. Otherwise you may form the habit of never properly joining the limbs together. Take care never to make the head turn in the same direction as the chest nor the arm move in the same direction as the leg; and if the head is turned towards the right shoulder, make all the parts lower on the left side than on the right; but if you make the chest prominent and the head turning on the left side, then make the parts on the right side higher than those on the left.

[McM., no. 121.]

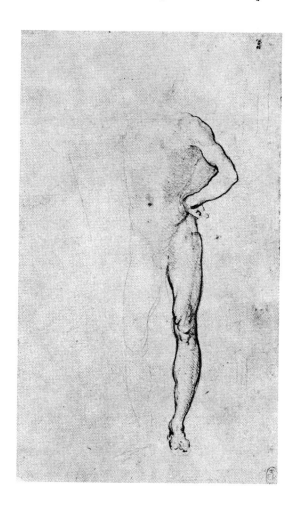

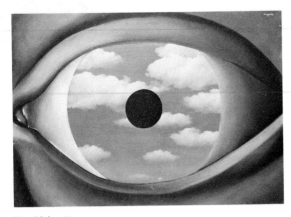

René Magritte,
The False Mirror,
1928, oil on canvas, cm. 54 x 81.

I think it is no small attraction in a painter to be able to give a pleasing air to his figures, and whoever is not naturally possessed of this grace may acquire it by study, as opportunity offers, in the following manner: be on the watch to take good parts of many beautiful faces of which the beautiful parts are established by general repute rather than by your own judgment, for you may deceive yourself by selecting faces that resemble your own, since it often seems that such similarities please us; and if you were ugly you would select faces that are not beautiful, and you would paint ugly faces as do many painters, whose painted figures often resemble that of their master; so therefore choose the beautiful ones as I tell you and fix them in your mind.

[McM., no. 276.]

First—the pupil of the eye contracts as the light reflected in it increases.

Second—the pupil of the eye expands as the brightness of day or any other light reflected in it grows less.

Third—the eye sees and knows objects of vision with greater intensity when the pupil is more dilated; and this is proved in the case of the nocturnal animals such as cats and others, and birds such as the owl and such like in which the pupil undergoes a great variation from large to small in the dark and in the light.

Fourth—the eye when placed in an illuminated atmosphere can discern the darkness within the windows of habitations which are themselves in light.

[MacC., p. 244, and cf. McM., no. 195.]

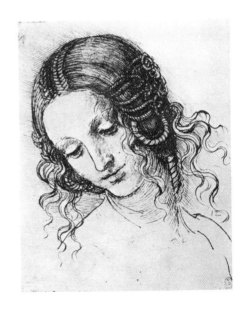

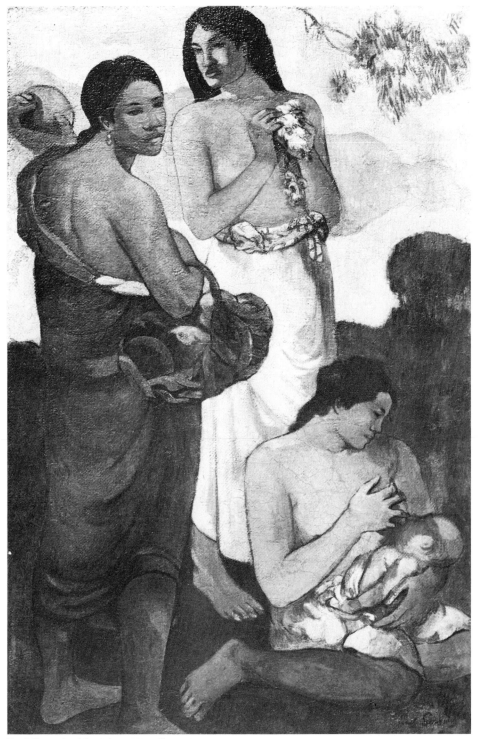

Paul Gauguin, *Maternity*, 1899, oil, cm. 94 x 59.5.

Affective gestures pointing to things near either in time or space should be made with the hand not very far from the body of the person pointing; and if these things are distant, the hand of the pointer should be more extended and the face turned toward the person to whom he is addressing the demonstration.

[McM., no. 412.]

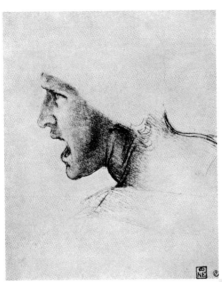

The good painter must depict two principal things to paint: namely, man and the intention of his mind. The first is easy, the second difficult, because it has to be represented by gestures and movements of the parts of the body, and this is to be learned from mutes who make such gestures better than anyone else.

[McM., no. 248.]

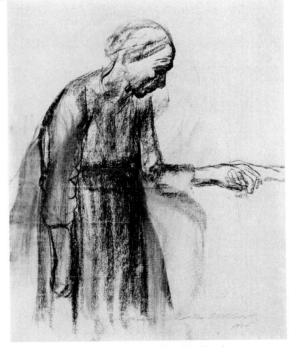

Käthe Kollwitz, *Woman Entrusts Herself to Death,* c. 1934, charcoal on paper, cm. 67.5 x 50.

George Bellows, *A Stag at Sharkey's*, 1909, oil, cm. 114.5 x 160

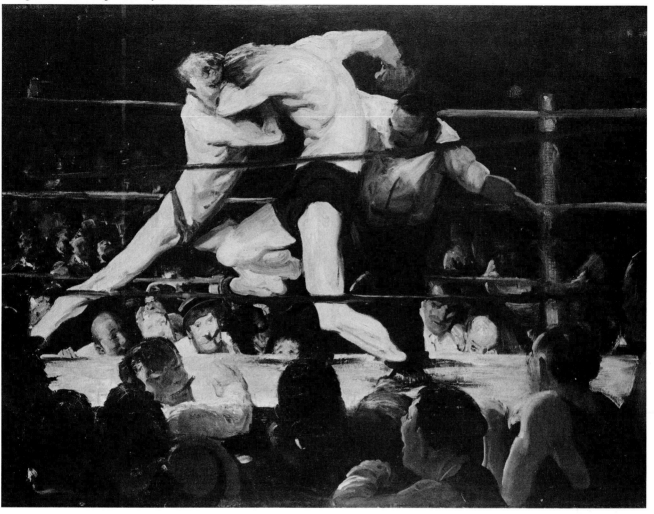

Let the poses of people and the parts of their
bodies be so disposed that they display the intent
of their minds.

[*McM., no. 399.*]

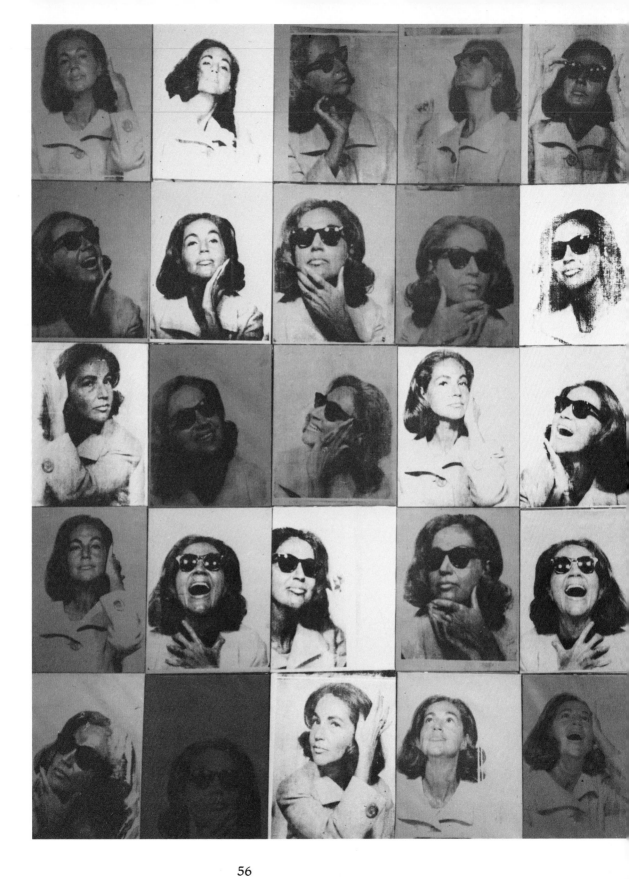

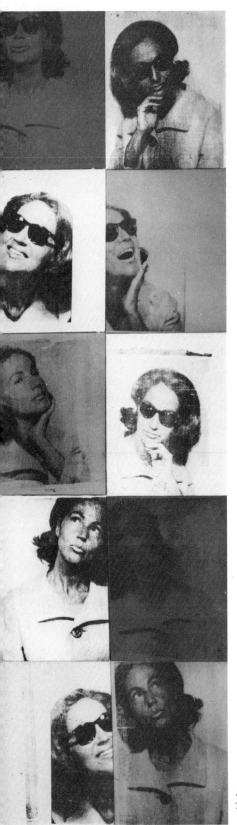

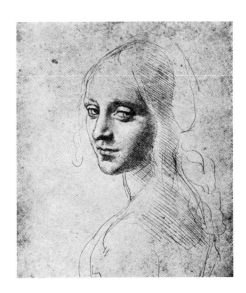

Make your faces so that they do not all have the same expression, as one sees with most painters, but give them different expressions, according to age, complexion, and good or bad character.
[McM., no. 414.]

Andy Warhol, *Portrait of Ethel Scull,*
1963, silkscreen enamel on canvas, 35 panels, each cm. 51 x 40.5.

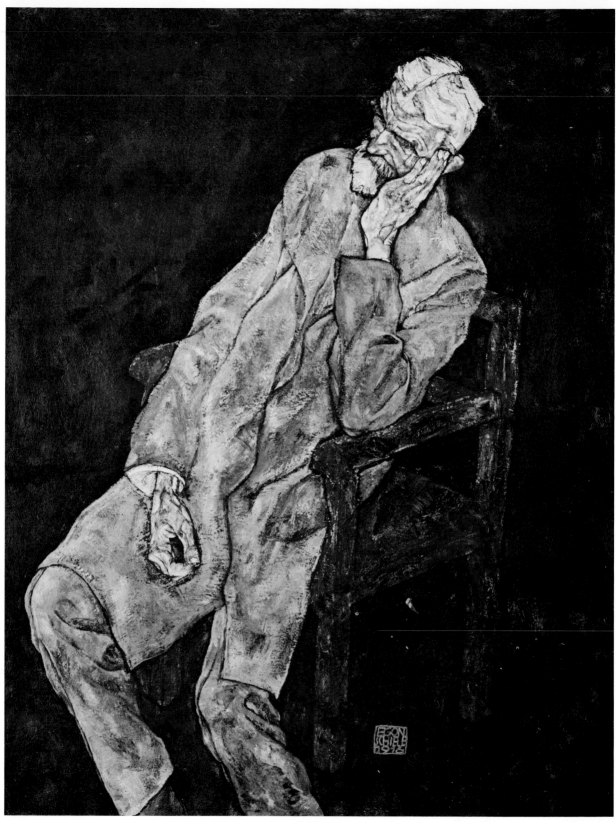

Egon Schiele, *Portrait of Johann Harms*, 1916, oil on canvas, cm. 138.5 x 108.

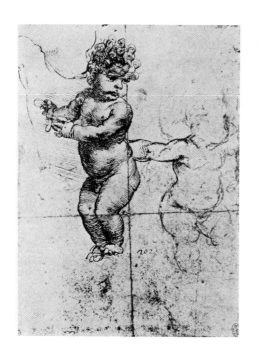

I remind you to pay great attention in making the limbs of your figures, so that they may not merely appear to harmonize with the size of the body but also with its age. So the limbs of youths should have few muscles and veins, and have a soft surface and be rounded and pleasing in color; in men they should be sinewy and full of muscles; in old men the surface should be wrinkled, and rough, and covered with veins, and with the sinews greatly protruding.

[*MacC., p. 889.*]

Little children when sitting should be represented with quick, irregular movements, and when they stand up, with timid and fearful movements.

[*McM., no. 252.*]

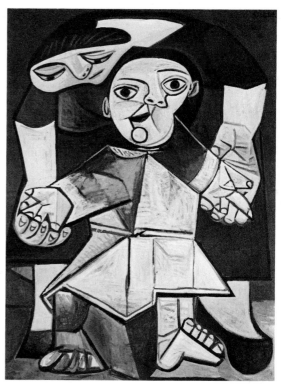

Pablo Picasso, *First Steps*, 1943, oil on canvas, cm. 130 x 97.

59

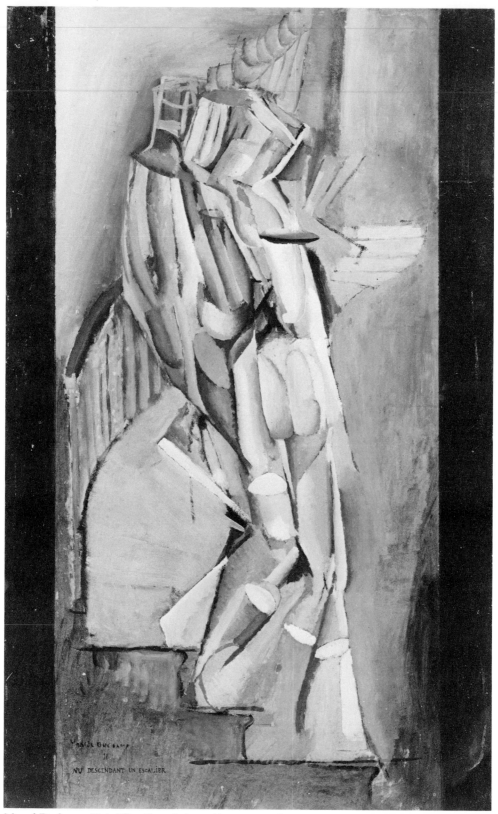

Marcel Duchamp, *Nude Descending a Staircase, No. 1*, 1911, oil, cm. 147 x 89.

The motions of animals are of two kinds, that is, motion in space and contained motion. Motion in space is when the animal moves from place to place, and contained motion is that which the animal makes within itself without change of place.

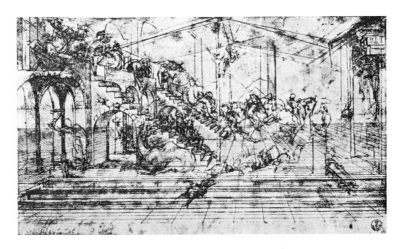

Motion in space is of three kinds, that is, ascending, descending, and motion on a level, and to these three are added two [qualifications]: that is, slowness and rapidity, and two others, that is, straight motion and tortuous motion, and then one more, that is, the motion of leaping. But contained motion is infinite, like the infinite actions in which, often not without danger to himself, a man engages. Motions are of three general kinds; that is, motion in space, simple contained motion, and the third, motion compounded of contained motion and motion in space. Slowness and rapidity ought not to be counted among motions in space but are incidental conditions of those motions.

Compound motions are infinite, and among them are: dancing, fencing, playing, sowing, plowing, and rowing; but rowing is really a simple contained motion, because contained motion made by man in rowing is not combined with man's motion in space, but the motion of the boat.

[McM., no. 355.]

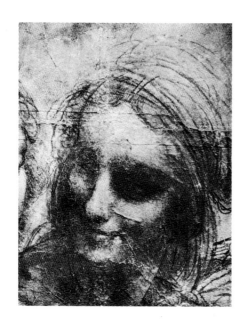

Never make heads straight on the shoulders, but turn them aside to the right or to the left, even though they look down, or upward, or straight ahead, because it is necessary for them to look lively and awake and not asleep. And do not depict the front or rear half of the whole person so that too much straightness is displayed, one half above or below the other half; and if you should wish to use stiff figures, do so only in portraying old people. . . .

[*McM.*, no. 385.]

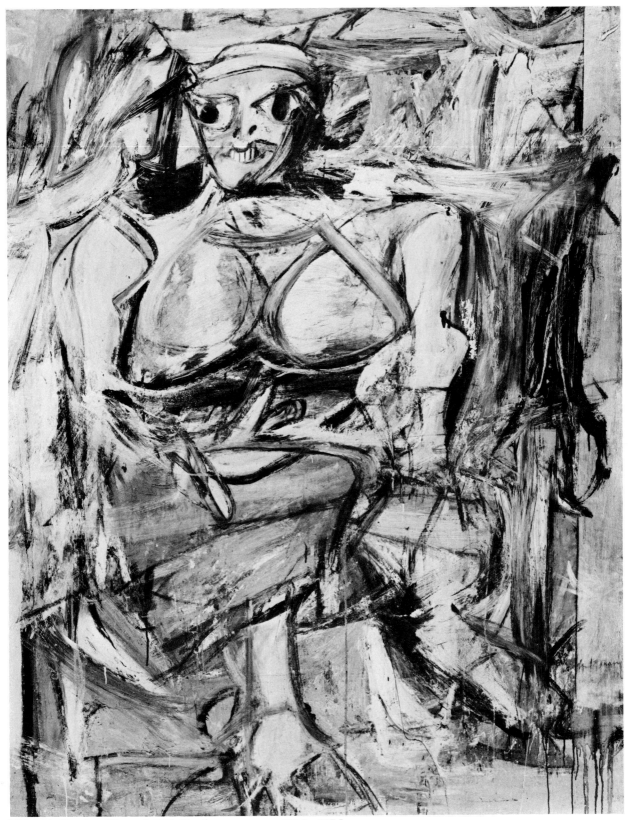

Willem de Kooning, *Woman, I*, 1950–52, oil on canvas, cm. 192.5 x 147.5.

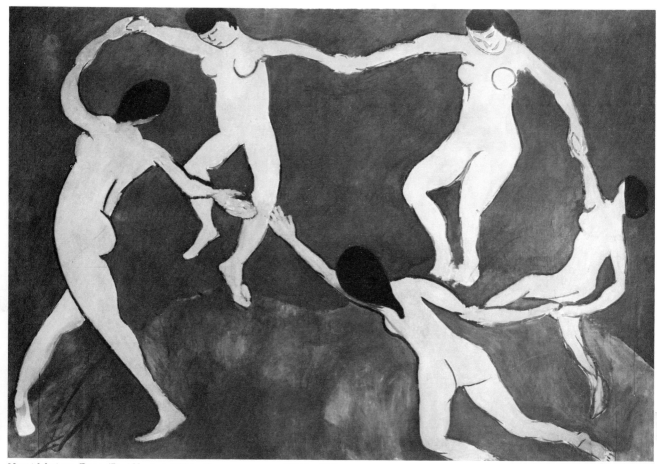

Henri Matisse, *Dance (First Version)*, 1909, oil on canvas, cm. 260.5 x 390.

As regards the arrangement of the limbs, you should bear in mind that when you wish to represent one who by some change has either to turn backwards or on one side, you must not make him move his feet and all his limbs in the same direction as he turns his head; but you should show the process spreading itself and taking effect over the four sets of joints, namely those of the foot, the knee, the hip, and the neck. . . .

[MacC., p. 892–93.]

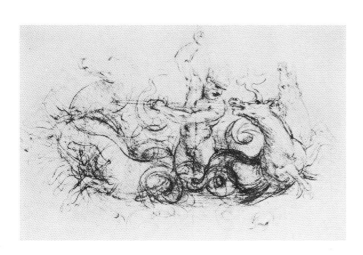

III.Subject Matter

For Leonardo history or narrative painting is the most significant category within a hierarchy that follows the precepts of Alberti, and one that has been observed in the academies virtually ever since. What may be less obvious is that a similar preference is not uncommon in twentieth-century painting. Consider, for example, the universal appeal of Picasso's *Guernica*, which must be defined as a history picture, in equal measure to Raphael's *School of Athens.* In his references to narrative pictures and in his advice to artists about them, Leonardo often raises general issues about painting, composition, variety, and complexity that are central to his art theory. Already in his *Adoration of the Magi* Leonardo includes the variety of elements that he recommends in writing, "so that the novelty and abundance attract people to it and delight the eye of the observer." A mixture of men and women of various ages in diverse costume or nude, children, animals, landscape, and buildings all appear in the painting, together with a battle scene involving horses in the background, an element difficult to understand within the context of the picture's theme.

Leonardo's advice about variety is actually a paraphrase from Alberti, and his *Adoration of the Magi* is heir to a long and illustrious rendering of the subject in Tuscan painting, which Leonardo elaborated into a scenographic drama. Nevertheless, Leonardo recognized the danger of crowding his compositions and confusing the spectator, a warning that he again may have derived from Alberti. In the *Last Supper* and in the *Battle of Anghiari* the diversity of the visual elements is tempered by his focused treatment of the theme and by limiting the number of actors to a bare minimum. In the *Last Supper*, for instance, few extraneous impulses detract from the main action—there is no dog or cat under the table (although certain copies show such a detail), no array of elaborately designed fabrics. Even the clothes of the principals are

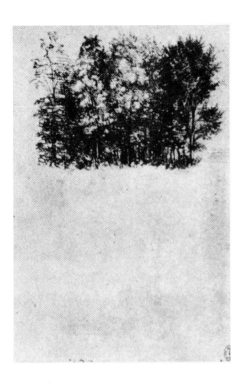

simplified, and the colors, or at least what is left of them, reveal the same restraint.

Narrative paintings offer greater visual and expressive possibilities than paintings of single figures, portraits, or still lifes, since they can and often do incorporate all of these elements. They also give the painter an opportunity to explore psychological dimensions, in which one figure acts upon and interacts with others or within a complex situation. The connotations of the myth or chronicle often serve to enrich the formal and purely aesthetic elements of the work. One can easily respond to Picasso's *Guernica* without knowing about the bombing that triggered its conception or the artist's political position during the Spanish Civil War. But Picasso's insights into the general theme of struggle, terror, and destruction are made even more powerful by an awareness of the specific circumstances surrounding the picture's conception.

Although pure landscape painting had not yet developed as a genre at the time that Leonardo was painting and writing—certainly not in Tuscany—Leonardo had a deep commitment to the depiction of nature. The first dated work that we have from his hand is a landscape drawing of 1473, which shows that even early in his career his concerns went beyond the requirements of an effective background for a Madonna or a portrait. Already he shows an appreciation of the fact that landscape has its own independent validity. Leonardo made some extraordinary landscape drawings, many rendered directly from nature, and others that seem more imagined than observed. The painted landscapes in the backgrounds of some of his paintings, on the other hand, have an unreal, even surreal, quality, remote from the kind of direct observation one expects from this master; nor are they consistent with many of his written observations about landscape. Although these background landscapes with huge mountains and deep valleys cut by meandering rivers are based on experience in the Alps, the effect is so dreamlike, so charged with fantasy, that one suspects that it is in the area of landscape treatment that Leonardo's art and theory are farthest apart. One might also ask if his figures too are more dreamlike and ethereal than he advocated in writing. The haunting qualities of the face of *Mona Lisa* or the *Madonna of the Rocks* are indeed distant from the naturalism employed by some of his contemporaries. When Leonardo advocates that landscapes be rendered when the sun is veiled by clouds and the light is not direct but diffused, is that not similar to his advice to paint figures in the late afternoon in a soft light? In his theoretical writings on landscape, however, Leonardo comes very close to the Impressionists because of his unfailing insistence on the power of observation. In a passage from the *Treatise* he seems to be describing Monet's or Renoir's paintings of the 1870s:

> . . . *if you portray* [*such*] *figures as being in the country, they are surrounded by a great quantity of light, when the sun is not covered. If the sun shines directly, their shadows will be very dark in comparison with the illuminated parts, and these will be shadows with definite edges, the original as well as the derivative ones. These shadows will be in little accord with the lights because the blue of the air illuminates one side, giving it a tinge of itself—this is quite manifested in white things— and that side which is illuminated by the sun takes on the color of the sun. This you will observe very readily when the sun falls to the horizon among the redness of the clouds, for those clouds are tinged with the color that illuminates them. The red of the clouds, together with the red of the sun, reddens that which is illuminated by*

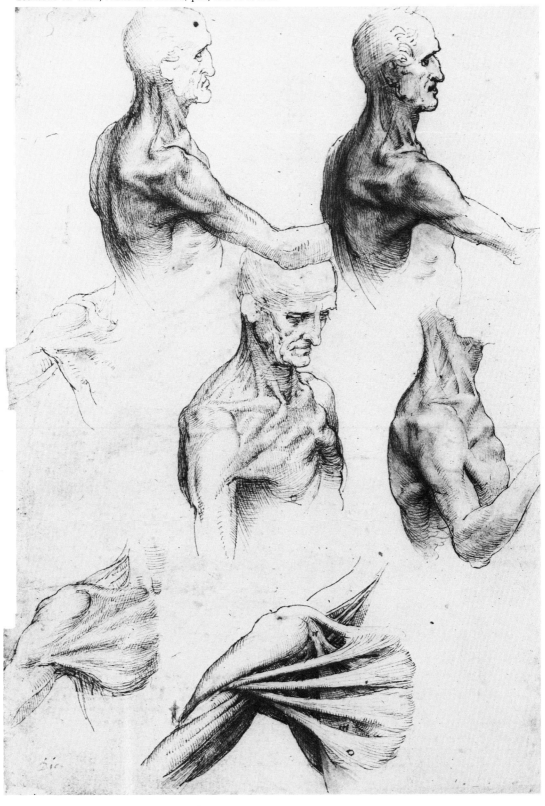

them. The side of bodies which does not face this
redness remains the color of the air, and whoever
sees such bodies judges them to be of two colors.
You cannot avoid showing the causes of such
shadows and lights, and making the shadows and
lights take on the color of their causes. If you do
not, your work is vain and false.

[McM., no. 140.]

Nor can one avoid conjuring up pictures by Cézanne when reading Leonardo, who advised:

O painter, when you make trees near at hand, re-
member that when your eye is somewhat below the
level of the tree you will be able to see some leaves
right side up and others on the reverse; and the
ones right side up will be a deeper blue to the de-
gree that they are seen more foreshortened, and
the same leaf will sometimes show partly right
side up and partly in reverse, and consequently
you must make it of two colors.

[MacC., p. 932.]

Another important aspect of painting, one that has occupied painters since the Renaissance and one with strong antique traditions, did not escape Leonardo's attention. "Fool-the-eye" painting, better known today as *trompe l'oeil,* is a technique in which the natural object is made indistinguishable from the painted object or at least in which the borderline between the two has been seriously disturbed. Lying behind the notion is perhaps Leonardo's proposition that the painter contends with and rivals nature. His anecdotes on the subject parallel those found in ancient writers, especially Pliny who describes a contest between the two painters:

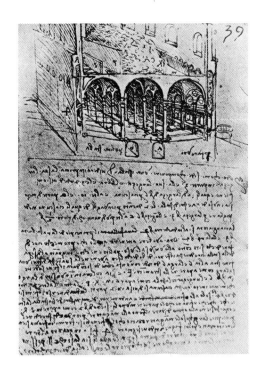

The last mentioned [Parrhasios] is reputed to have entered into a contest with Zeuxis, and when the latter depicted some grapes with such success that birds flew up to the scene, he then depicted a linen curtain with such verisimilitude that Zeuxis, puffed up with pride by the verdict of the birds, eventually requested that the curtain be removed and his picture shown, and, when he understood his error, conceded with sincere modesty, because he himself had only deceived birds, but Parrhasios had deceived him, an artist. It was said that afterwards Zeuxis painted a picture of a boy carrying grapes, and when the birds flew up to them, he approached the work and, in irritation with it, said, "I have painted the grapes better than the boy, for if I had rendered him perfectly, the birds would have been afraid."

[Pliny, Natural History, XXXV, 61.]

While Leonardo expresses considerable interest in "fool-the-eye" painting, none of his extant works exhibits this quality, but a long tradition of veristic still lifes indicates the appeal of this genre.

Ronald B. Kitaj, *The Ohio Gang,* oil and crayon on canvas, cm. 183 x 183.5.

I say [also] that in narrative paintings one should mingle direct contraries close by, because they produce strong contrasts with one another, and all the more so when they are very close together; that is, the ugly next to the beautiful, the big to the small, the old to the young, the strong to the weak; in this way you will vary as much as possible and close by.

[McM., no. 271.]

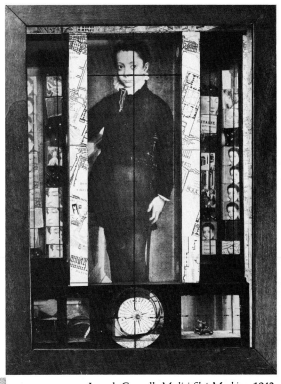

Joseph Cornell, *Medici Slot Machine*, 1942,
construction, cm. 34.5 x 30.5 x 11.

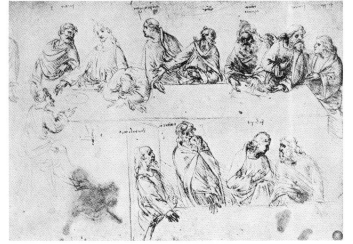

Pablo Picasso,
Combat of Perseus and Phineus over Andromeda,
1931, etching, cm. 22 x 17.

*In a history painting, the dignity and decorum of
a prince or sage should be maintained, it is pro-
posed, by separating him and setting him entirely
apart from the tumult of the crowd.*
[McM., no. 272.]

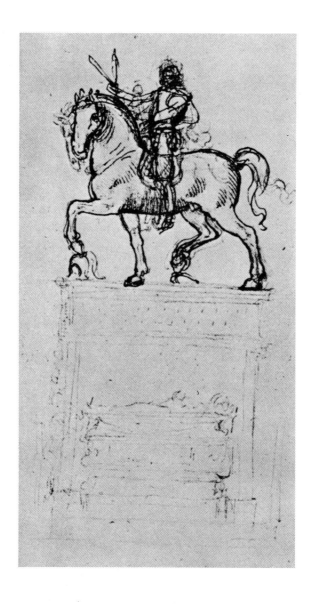

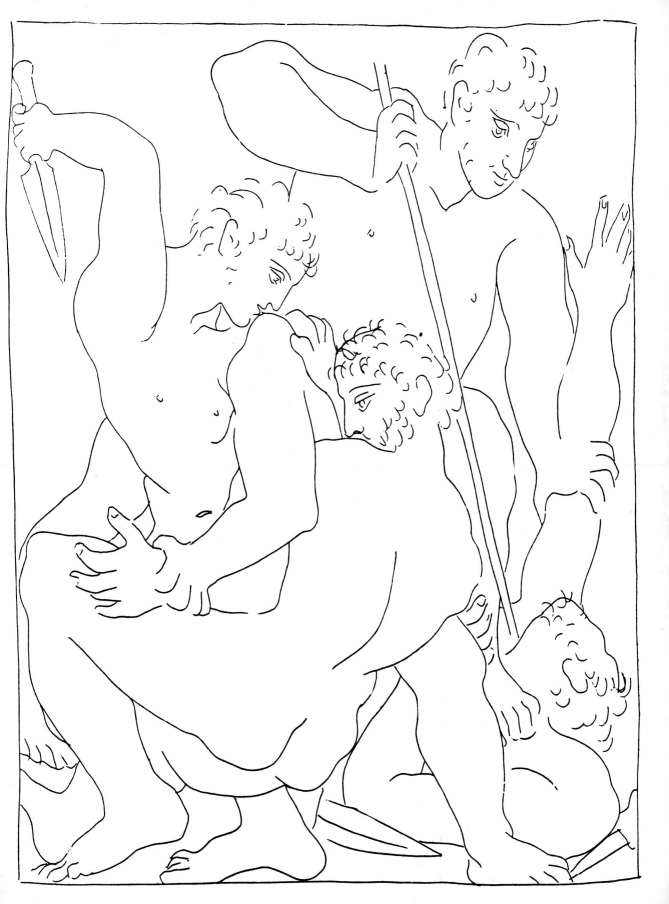

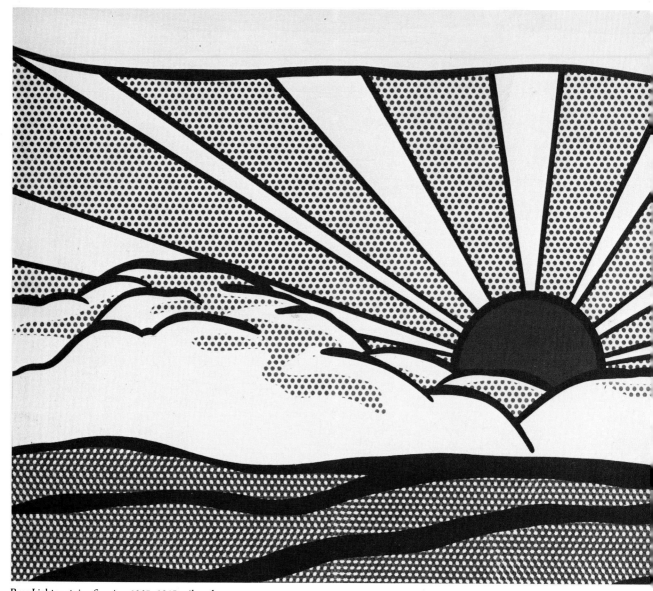

Roy Lichtenstein, *Sunrise, 1965*, 1965, oil and magna on canvas, cm. 91.5 x 172.5.

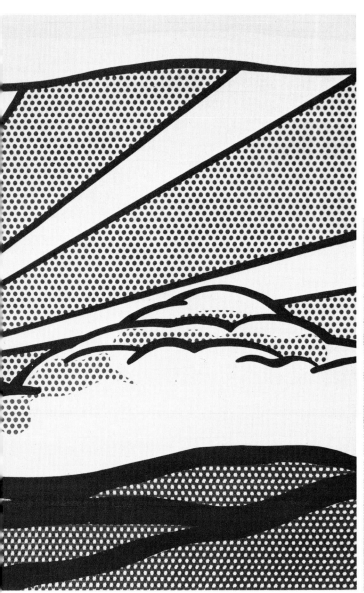

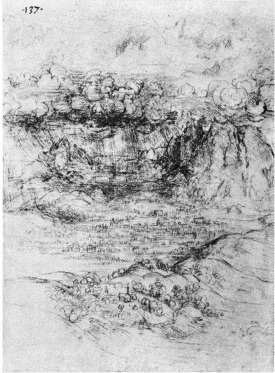

Never will the colors, the vivacity and the clarity of painted landscapes equal natural landscapes illuminated by the sun, unless the painted landscapes are also illuminated by the sun.

[McM., no. 192.]

One sees clearly that the part of the atmosphere which lies nearest ground level is denser than the rest, and that the higher it rises the thinner and more transparent it becomes. In the case of the large and lofty objects which are some distance away from you, their lower parts will be little seen, because you see them on a line that passes through the thickest and densest portion of the atmosphere. . . .

[McM., no. 230.]

Vincent van Gogh, *The Washerwomen*, 1888, ink.

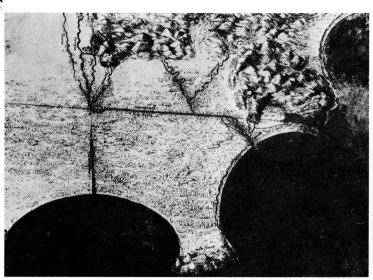

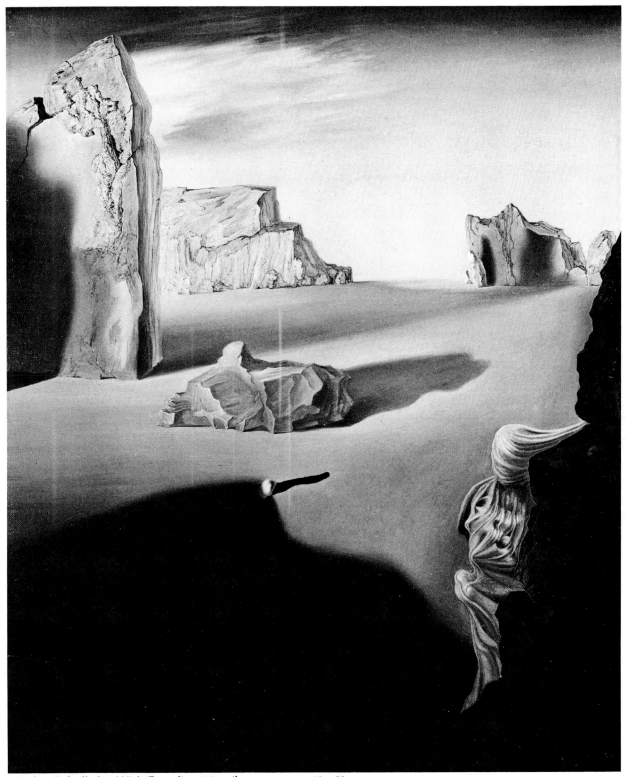

Salvadore Dali, *Shades of Night Descending*, 1931, oil on canvas, cm. 61 x 50.

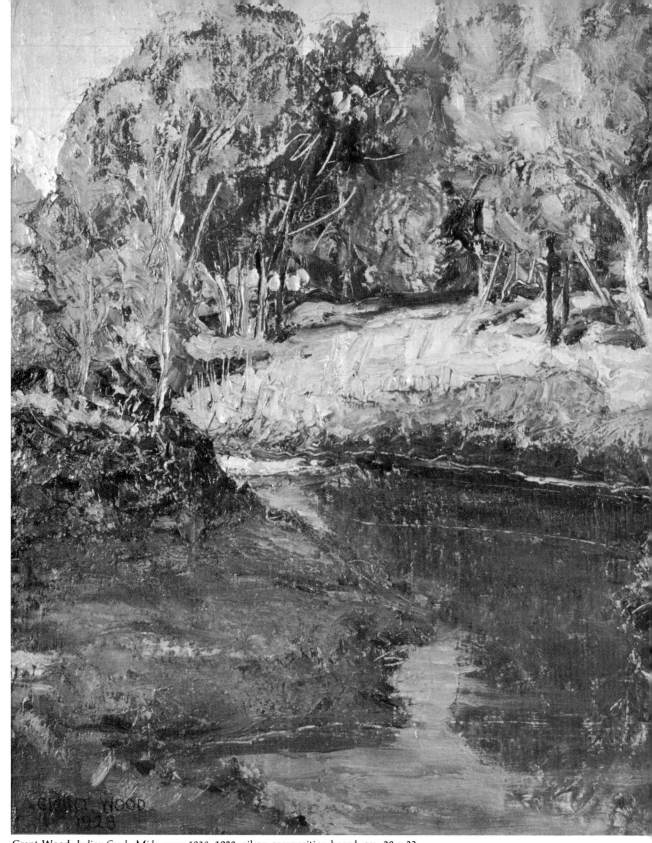

Grant Wood, *Indian Creek, Midsummer 1928*, 1928, oil on composition board, cm. 38 x 33.

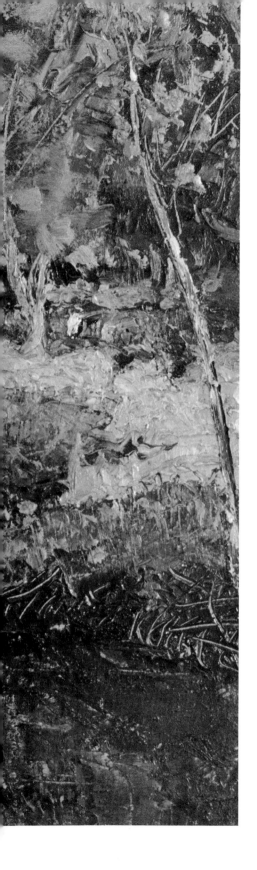

The outlines of the structure of trees against the luminous atmosphere, as they are more remote, approach the spherical more closely in their shape, and as they are nearer, so they display a greater divergence from the spherical form. . . .

Every object in shadow—be it of whatever shape you please—will at a great distance appear to be spherical. . . .

[MacC., p. 938.]

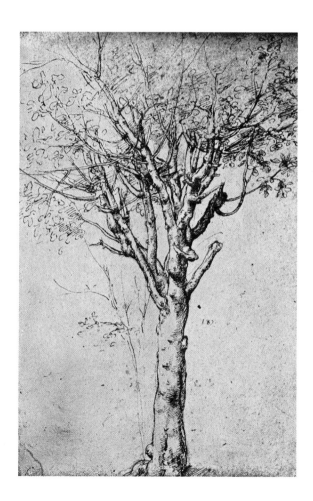

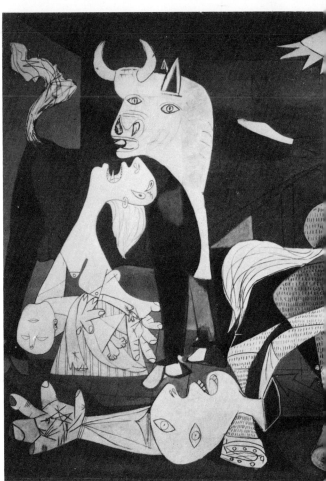

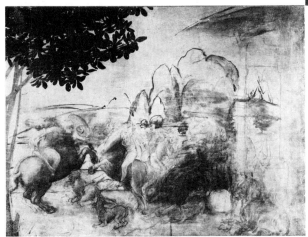

Let the painter composing narrative pictures take
pleasure in wealth and variety, and avoid repeating any part that occurs in it, so that the unique-
ness and abundance attract people to it and
delight the eye of the observer. I say that a narrative painting requires (depending on the scene),
wherever the eye falls, a mixture of men of diverse
appearances, of diverse ages and dress, combined
together with women, children, dogs, horses, buildings, fields, and hills.

[McM., no. 268.]

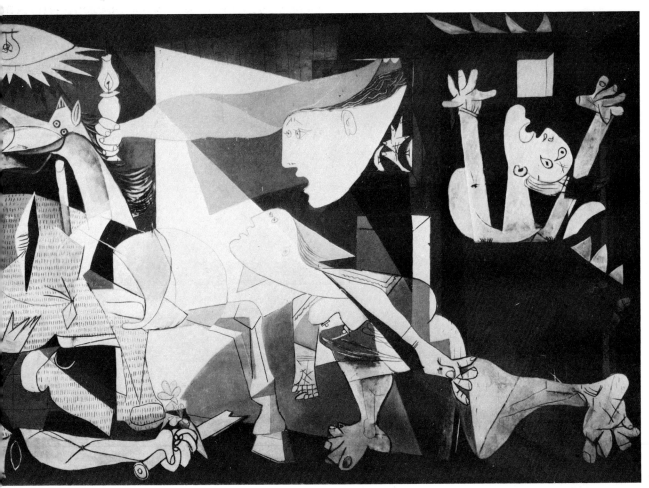

Pablo Picasso, *Guernica*, 1937, oil on canvas, cm. 349 x 776.5.

IV. Techniques for Representation

Within the world of Leonardo's ideas the separation of concepts dealing with color from those dealing with light and shadow is virtually impossible. In practice Leonardo appears to have been more precocious, innovative, and successful in treating light and shadow than in handling color: his paintings often may be taken as exercises in the use of *chiaroscuro* to build form. He also employed contrasts of light and shadow to establish relationships between figures and other elements in his paintings. As is well demonstrated by the *Adoration of the Magi*, these two aspects of light and shadow are fundamental for Leonardo. Only after laying in the entire composition and working out the overall lighting and the light and shadow within the individual figures did Leonardo apply his color. He never did arrive at that point with the *Adoration*, which remains unfinished and nearly monochromatic. In the *Mona Lisa*, on the other hand, where the use of light and shadow to establish form is achieved perfectly, there is very little color *per se*. Nevertheless, I believe that Leonardo was far more of a colorist than is commonly thought. He describes how to obtain the maximum effect of colors:

> For those colors that you wish to be beautiful, first prepare a very white ground, this I say with regard to transparent colors, for a bright ground is not an advantage to those that are not transparent. An example of this is shown by colored pieces of glass which when they are held between the eye and the luminous air, display great beauty, but which they do not have when the air behind them is shadowy air or some other obscurity.
>
> [McM., no. 191.]

Unfortunately, however, Leonardo left so few paintings that one has very little to go on to form an accurate judg-

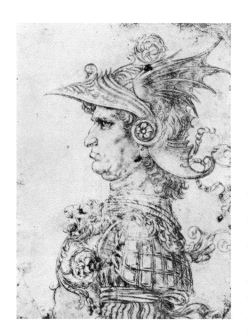

ment, and what has come down to us has suffered radically. The *Last Supper*—in which color was surely an important factor—is such a ruin that little can be said about how it looked immediately after completion and the color cannot be reconstructed in any sensible way.

Since Leonardo often failed to finish his works, and since the application of color was among the final steps within his working procedure, his pictures seem relatively colorless. Even the *Mona Lisa*, to which Leonardo seems to have been so deeply attached that he carried it around with him on his travels, may not actually be "finished." It probably had greater coloristic appeal than the painting now holds in the Louvre. In fact a wider range of color in the *Mona Lisa* may still rest within the picture but a vigorous restoration of the most famous painted image in Western art would simply be too risky. The *Mona Lisa* does, however, beautifully illustrate Leonardo's advice to paint in the half light of late afternoon, when the hues become less obvious and more subtle. He also observes:

> *A very high degree of grace in the shadows and in the lights is added to the faces of those who sit at the doorways of houses that are dark, where the eyes of the observer see the shadowed part of such a face darkened by the shadows of the aforementioned house, and see the illuminated part of that face with added brightness which the brilliance of the air gives it. Through this increase in the shadows and lights the face has great relief; on the illuminated side the shadows are almost indistinguishable, and on the dark side, the lights are almost indistinguishable. From such a representation and increase of shadows and lights, the face acquires considerable beauty.*
>
> [*McM., no.137.*]

If Leonardo's application of his color theory is difficult to demonstrate, these ideas about color have a remarkably modern ring. Since he based them on the direct observation of nature, he seems to predict the work of late-nineteenth-century masters. Nor does Leonardo separate from his concern with color the concept of perspective. He says:

> Perspective, to the extent that it relates to painting, is divided into three principal parts: the first is that of diminution which gives the dimensions of bodies at different distances; and the second is that which treats of the diminution of the intensity of colors of such bodies; the third is that which diminishes the perceptibility of those bodies at different distances.
>
> [McM., no. 484.]

The introduction of mathematically based perspective, which is found for the first time in Masaccio's paintings of the 1420s, left an indelible mark on Western art. Perspective as developed by Brunelleschi and as utilized by Donatello, Uccello, and Piero della Francesca, to mention a few early practitioners, was refined in the following generation so that by Leonardo's time it was no longer a novelty. Perspective had been adopted, with varying degrees of success, by all painters. As was the case with the study of human anatomy, Leonardo's predecessors had established many of the ground rules to set the stage for Leonardo and his contemporaries to formularize the study of perspective for artistic purposes.

For some modern artists the perspective system that has been used through the centuries has been a restrictive convention, one that must be overturned by severe modification or complete rejection. Around the turn of the twentieth century alternatives to traditional spatial rea-

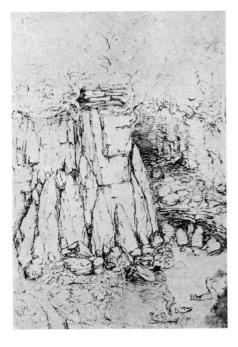

soning were being recognized in the arts of the Far East, Africa, and pre-Columbian America. Past Western art was found to offer alternatives as well, especially in pre-Renaissance painting and the images rendered by children. While some artists quickly adopted and developed the new options, the erosion of the Renaissance system of perspective has never been absolute, and many artists still rely on the rationalism exemplified by Leonardo's perspective.

Whether sublimated, rejected, or modified, the fifteenth-century concept of perspective remains an important ingredient of twentieth-century visual habits. Furthermore, the recent popularity of photography and the interest in the history of photography, together with the visual impact of films and television, have, if anything, reinforced the space-creating effects of perspective as developed in Leonardo's time. Indeed, for Leonardo perspective was an indispensable instrument for the correct depiction of the world on a two-dimensional surface—the vehicle whereby all of nature's phenomena can be recorded and thereby analyzed and understood. By means of perspective, a painting became a window to the world.

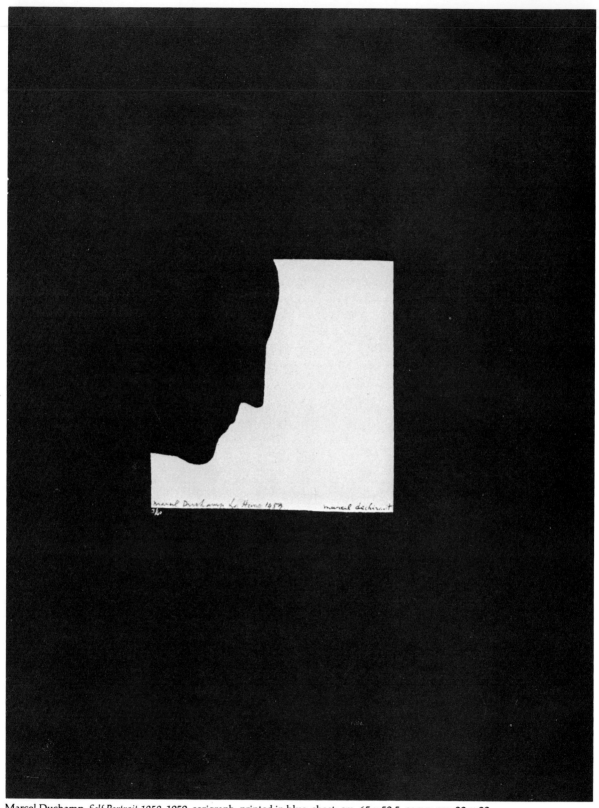

Marcel Duchamp, *Self Portrait 1959*, 1959, serigraph, printed in blue, sheet: cm. 65 x 50.5, comp: cm. 20 x 20.

*Greater analysis and ability are required to depict
the outlines of bodies than shadows and lights, because the outlines of parts of the body that are not
pliable are immutable and always the same, while
the location and quantity and quality of shadows
is infinite.*

[*McM., no. 106.*]

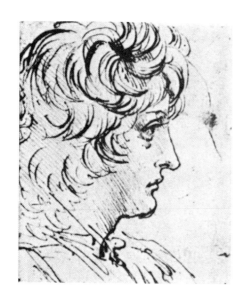

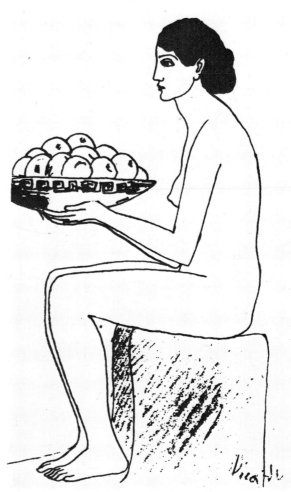

Pablo Picasso, *Nude Woman with Basket of Fruit*,
1902–1903, pen.

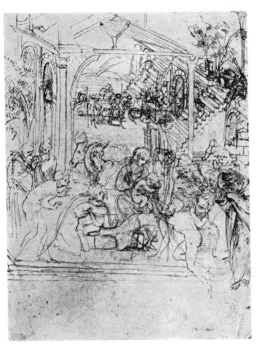

Perspective is a rational demonstration whereby experience confirms how all things transmit their images to the eye by pyramidal lines. By pyramidal lines I mean those which start from the extremities of the surface of bodies and by gradually converging from a distance arrive at the same point; the said point being, as I shall show, in this particular case located in the eye which is the universal judge of all objects. . . .

[MacC., p. 993.]

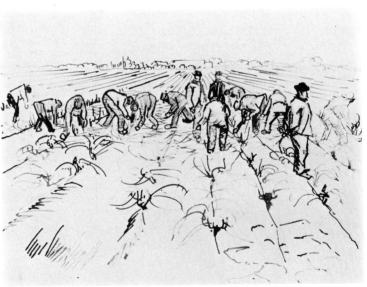

Vincent van Gogh, *Picking Peas*, Auvers period, pen.

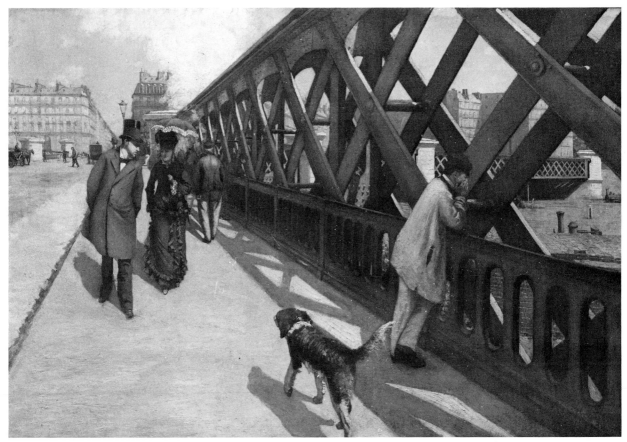

Gustave Caillebotte, *Le Pont de l'Europe*, 1876, oil, cm. 125 x 180.

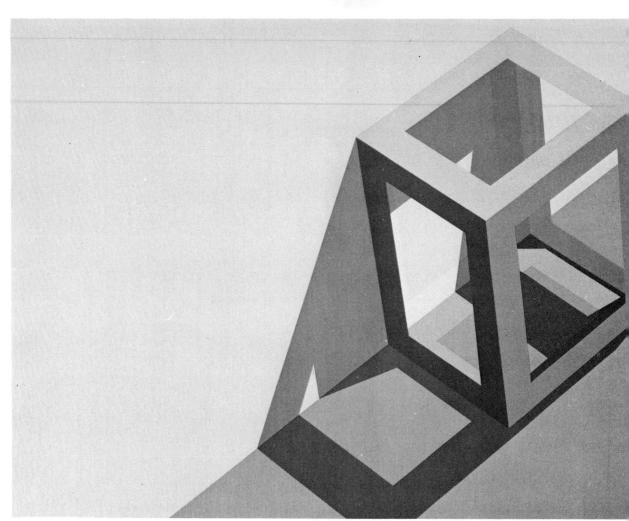

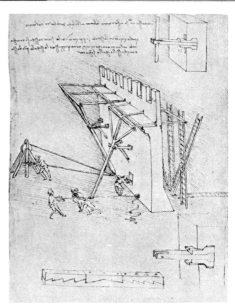

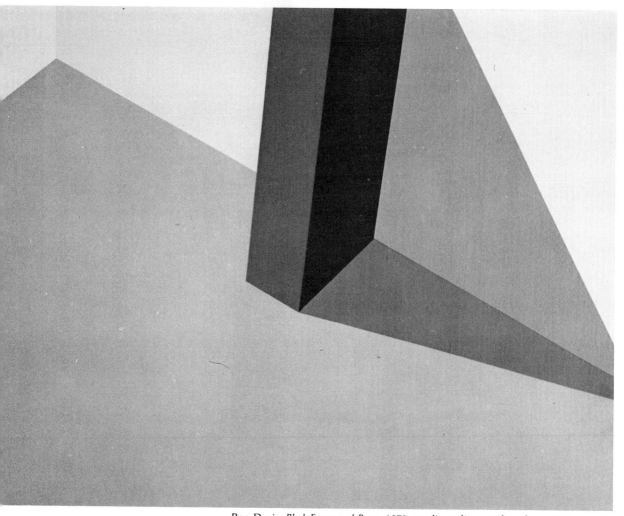

Ron Davis, *Block Frame and Beam*, 1973, acrylic on linen on board, cm. 40.5 x 106.5.

*Perspective is nothing else than the seeing of an
object behind a sheet of glass, smooth and quite
transparent, on the surface of which all the things
may be marked that are behind this glass; these
things approach the point of the eye in pyramids
and these pyramids are cut by the said glass.*
[*MacC., p. 993.*]

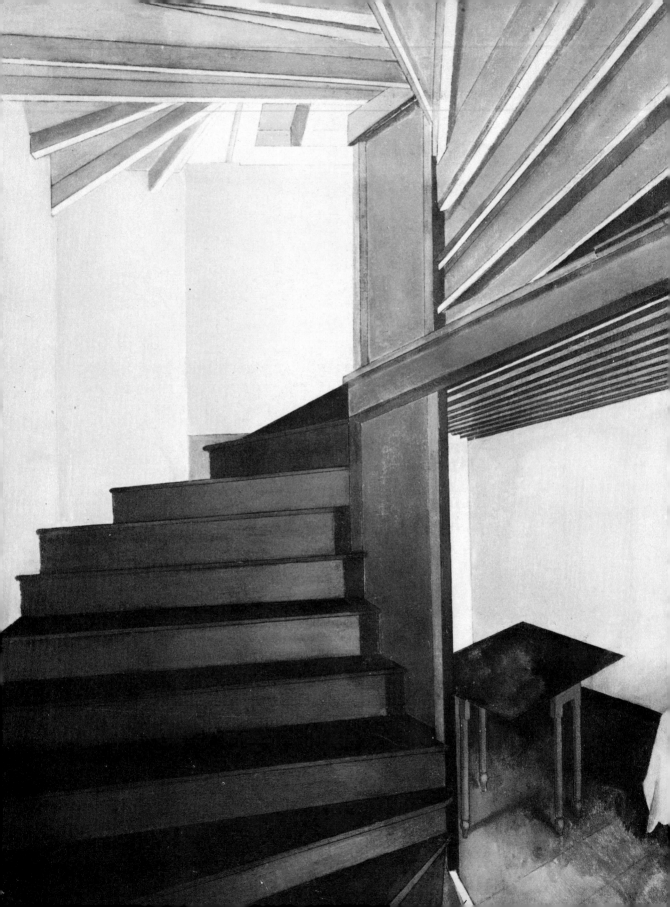

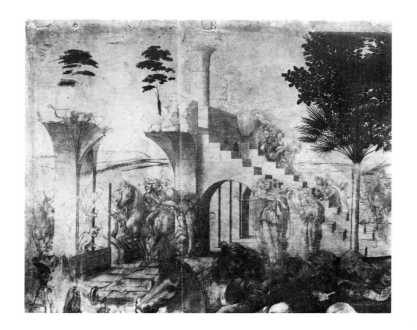

*The perspective by means of which a thing is rep-
resented will be better understood when it is seen
from the viewpoint at which it was drawn. . . .*
                        [*MacC., p. 995; Ms.
                        A, fol. 40v.*]

Perspective, to the extent that it relates to painting, is divided into three principal parts; the first is that of diminution which gives dimensions of bodies at different distances; and the second is that which treats of the diminution of the intensity of colors of such bodies; the third is that which diminishes the perceptibility of those bodies at different distances.

[McM., no. 484.]

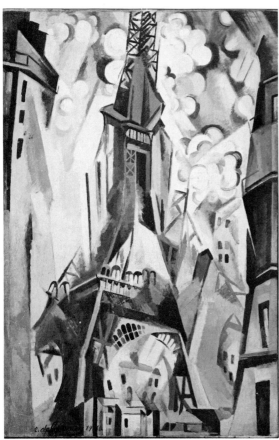

Robert Delaunay, *La Tour Eiffel*, 1910–1911, oil on canvas, cm. 195.5 x 129.

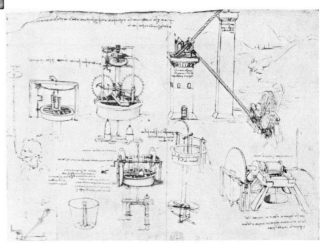

Georges Seurat, *A Sunday Afternoon at the Grande Jatte*, 1885, oil on canvas, cm. 70.49 × 104.14.

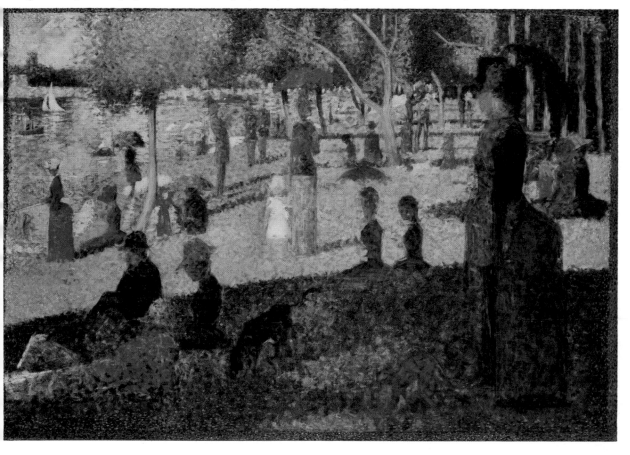

A shaded body will appear of less size when it is surrounded by a very luminous background, and a luminous body will show itself greater when it is set against a darker background: . . . as is shown in the heights of buildings at night when there are flashes of lightning behind, that the building loses a part of its height. And from this results that those buildings seem larger when there is mist or at night than when the air is clear and illuminated.

[MacC., p. 948.]

Franz Kline, *Painting #7, 1952*, 1952, oil on canvas, cm. 146.05 × 207.65.

Of colors of equal whiteness, that will seem most dazzling which is on the darkest background, and black will seem most intense when it is against a background of greater whiteness.

Red also will seem most vivid when against a yellow background, and so in like manner with all the colors when set against those which present the sharpest contrasts.

[MacC., p. 921.]

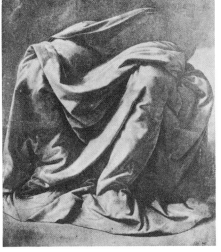

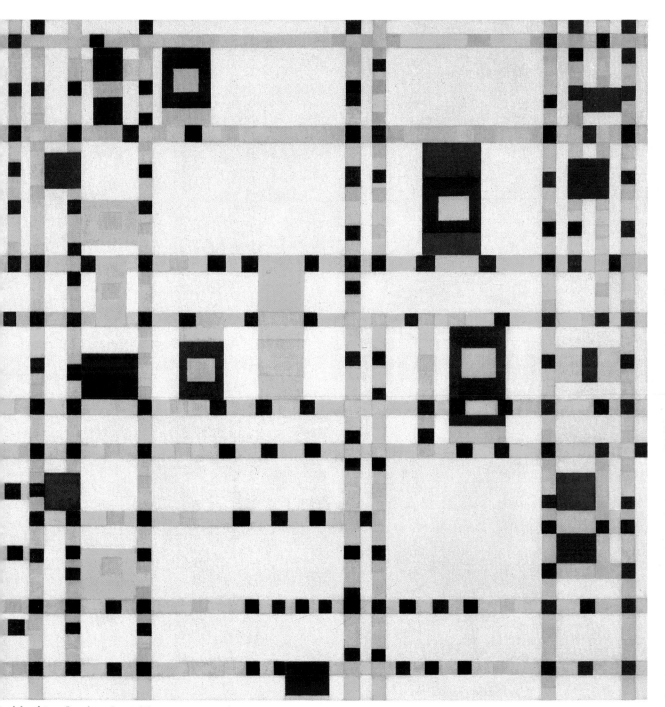

et Mondrian, *Broadway Boogie Woogie*, 1942–43, oil on canvas, cm. 127 × 127.

Jim Dine, *Double Isometric Self-Portrait (Serape)*, 1964, oil with objects, cm. 144.46 × 214.63.

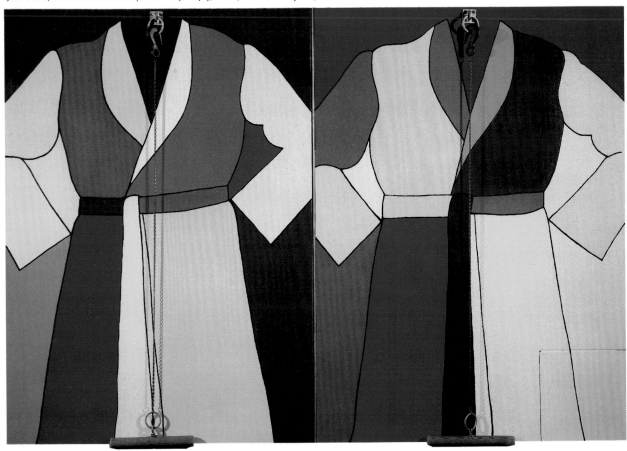

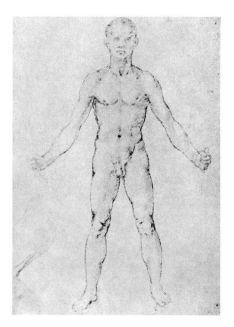

Ad Reinhardt, *Number 17—1953*, 1953, oil and tempera, cm. 197.49 × 197.49.

Black is like a broken vessel, which is deprived of
the capacity to contain anything [i.e., color].
                    [*McM., no. 205.*]

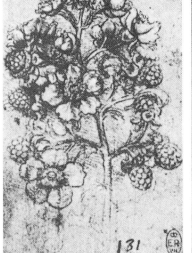

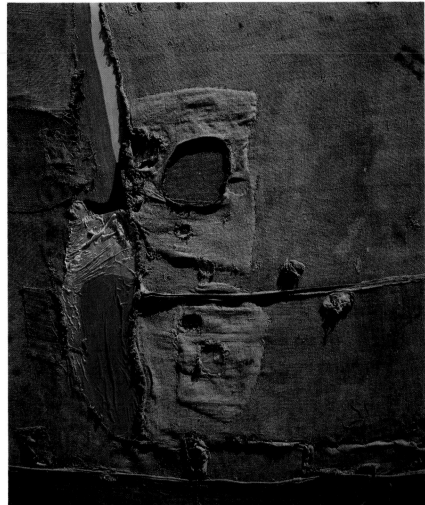

Alberto Burri, *Sacco*, 1953, mixed media, cm. 100 × 86.

*That body will show its true color most whose
surface is least polished and smooth.*

*This is seen in linen cloths and in the leaves of
grass and trees which are fuzzy, and where no
luster can be created. There, by the nature of
things, objects cannot be reflected, so that they
must render to the eye only the true color. . . .*
                                    [*McM., no. 209.*]

Wassily Kandinsky, *Autumn*, 1911, oil, cm. 71.12 × 99.06.

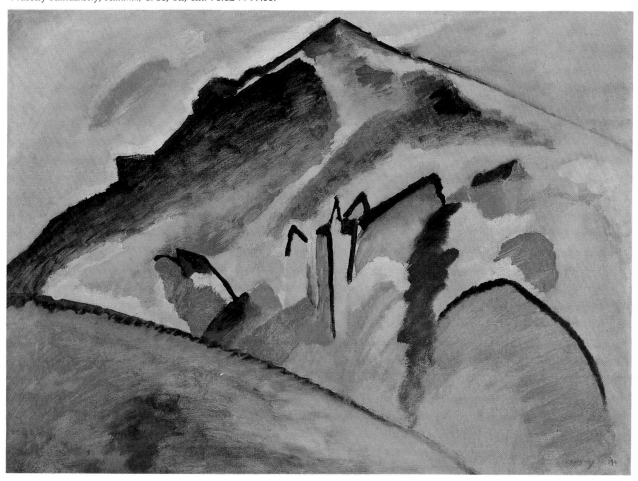

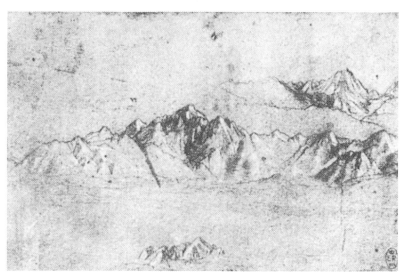

Credits

Leonardo da Vinci Illustrations

Pages 1, 3, 43, 49, 90, and 98, courtesy of the Louvre, Paris. *Pages 4, 5, 31, 39, 61, 82, and 95*, courtesy of the Uffizi Gallery, Florence. *Pages 7, 9, 11, 12, 15, 19, 20, 21, 23, 24, 27, 28, 29, 33, 35, 36, 40, 44, 47, 51, 52, 59, 65, 67, 69, 74, 77, 78, 81, 87, 89, 96, 100, 102, and 103*, courtesy of the Royal Library, Windsor. *Pages 16 and 85*, courtesy of the British Museum, London. *Page 54*, courtesy of the Museum of Fine Arts, Boston. *Page 57*, courtesy of the Royal Library, Turin. *Page 62*, courtesy of the Royal Academy of Arts, London. *Page 71*, courtesy of Institut de France, Paris. *Page 73*, courtesy of the Academy, Venice. *Page 92*, courtesy of the Ambrosiana, Milan.

Modern Illustrations

Pages 2 and 49, Courtauld Institute, London. *Pages 81 and 95*, Uffizi Gallery, Florence. *Pages 34, 58, and 98*, Solomon R. Guggenheim Museum, New York. *Page 37*, Collection of the Museum of Modern Art, New York. Acquired through the Lillie P. Bliss Bequest. *Page 38*, National Gallery of Art, Washington, D.C. Gift of the Avalon Foundation 1956. *Page 40*, Woodner Collection. Photo: Sam Salz. *Page 41*, Private collection. Photo: Bulloz. *Page 48*, Collection of the Museum of Modern Art, New York. Lillie P. Bliss Collection. *Page 50*, Sterling and Francine Clark Art Institute, Williamstown, Massachusetts. *Pages 52 and 63*, Collection of the Museum of Modern Art, New York. Purchase. *Page 53*, photo courtesy of Wildenstein & Co., Inc. Photo: Soichi Sunami. *Page 54*, Collection of Mr. and Mrs. Jacob M. Kaplan, New York. *Page 55*, Cleveland Museum of Art. *Page 56*, Private collection, New York. Photo: Eric Pollitzer. *Page 59*, Yale University Art Gallery, New Haven, Connecticut. Gift of Stephen C. Clark. *Page 60*, Philadelphia Museum of Art. Louise and Walter Arensberg Collection. *Page 64*, Collection of the Museum of Modern Art, New York. Gift of Nelson A. Rockefeller in honor of Alfred H. Barr, Jr. Photo: Eric Pollitzer. *Page 72*, Collection of the Museum of Modern Art, New York. Philip Johnson Fund. *Page 73*, Solomon R. Guggenheim Museum, New York. Bernard J. Reis Collection. *Page 75*, Collection of the Museum of Modern Art, New York. Gift of James Thrall Soby. *Page 76*, Leo Castelli Gallery. Photo: Rudolph Burckhardt. *Page 78*, Kröller-Müller State Museum, Otterlo. *Page 79*, Dali Museum, Cleveland. Collection of Mr. and Mrs. A. Reynolds Morse. *Page 80*, Estate of Mrs. Arthur Erskine, Cedar Rapids, Iowa. *Page 83*, on extended loan to the Museum of Modern Art, New York. From the artist's estate. *Page 88*, Collection of the Museum of Modern Art, New York. Gift of Lang Charities, Inc. *Page 89*, Collection Sunger. *Page 90*, Collection Vincent W. van Gogh, Laren. *Page 91*, Musée Petit Palais, Paris. *Pages 92–93*, Collection of United Jewish Appeal. Photo: Frank J. Thomas. *Page 94*, Hirshhorn Museum and Sculpture Garden, Washington, D.C. *Page 96*, Künstmuseum, Basel. *Page 97*, Metropolitan Museum of Art, New York. Bequest of Samuel A. Lewisohn, 1951. *Page 98*, Martha Jackson Galleries, New York. *Page 99*, Collection of the Museum of Modern Art, New York. Given anonymously. *Page 100*, Collection of Mrs. Helen W. Benjamin. Courtesy Whitney Museum of American Art, New York. *Page 101*, Collection of the Whitney Museum of American Art, New York. *Page 102*, Collection of the artist. Photo: Aurelio Amendola. *Page 103*, Collection of Mrs. Lora F. Mark, Chicago.